COVER DOG

Canadian Champion Chumulari Ying-Ying, the glorious gold and white Shih Tzu, owned by the Reverend and Mrs. D. Allan Easton, from stock that is directly descended from the last lion dogs known to have been born in the Peking Imperial Palace.

Our cover dog has carved himself a permanent niche in breed history! At the New Brunswick Kennel Club show in New Jersey on September 1st, 1969, on the first day Shih Tzu were allowed to compete as a recognized breed in American dog shows, Ch. Chumulari Ying-Ying was Best of Breed under judge Alva Rosenberg, and first in the Toy Group and on to Best in Show under judge James W. Trullinger. He was handled to this spectacular win by Mr. John J. Marsh. This is the first time in the history of American dog shows that a Best in Show win was made by a newly recognized breed its first time out in regular competition.

Cover water color portrait by Ernest H. Hart
from a Tauskey photograph.

PHOTO CREDITS

Rudolph Tauskey, Robert R. Blankley, D. Allan Easton, The China Chronicle, Danish Information Agency, Jay Reed–The Milwaukee Journal, Andreus, C. M. Cook & Son, Walter Guiver, Frans Kramer, Thomas Fall, Richard W. Schlott, 3rd, Modern Photographers (Saudi Arabia), Furman Studio, Hasbrouck Studio, Christer Söderlund, Bill Francis, Harisch Studio, Theodore S. Sodrosky, Erich Gross, Vinell Studios, Newark Evening News, The Anchorage Times, Gunzleman Studios, Koraen Photography, Evelyn Shafer, Jay Florian Mitchell, William P. Gilbert, Aftonbladen Bildservice, Stu Wainwright.

The authors wish to express special thanks to Mr. Per-Axel Lindblom, Shih Tzu fancier and accomplished photographer, for many of the portraits and "how-to" photographs included in this book. His contribution to the literature on the breed is a noteworthy one and is most sincerely appreciated.

Distributed in the U.S. by T.F.H. Publications, Inc., 211 West Sylvania Avenue, P.O. Box 427, Neptune, NJ 07753; in England by T.F.H. (Gt. Britain) Ltd., 13 Nutley Lane, Reigate, Surrey; in Canada to the book store and library trade by Beaverbooks, Ltd., 150 Lesmill Road, Don Mills, Ontario M38 2T5, Canada; in Canada to the pet trde by Rolf C. Hagen Ltd., 3225 Sartelon Street, Montreal 382, Quebec; in Southeast Asia by Y.W. Ong, 9 Lorong 36 Geylang, Singapore 14; in Australia and the South Pacific by Pet Imports Pty. Ltd., P.O. Box 149, Brookvale 2100, N.S.W. Australia; in South Africa by Valid Agencies, P.O. Box 51901, Randburg 2125 South Africa, Published by T.F.H. Publications, Inc., Ltd, the British Crown Colony of Hong Kong.

THIS IS
THE SHIH TZU

by The Reverend D. Allan Easton
and
Joan McDonald Brearley

DEDICATION

This book is dedicated to the delightful little breed that has charmed and won the hearts of dog lovers down through the ages from ancient Chinese dynasties to our modern-day sophisticated dog fanciers. Long may they reign!

SHIH TZU is pronounced SHID ZOO

CONTENTS

Frontispiece: Chumulari Trari, owned and bred by Rev. and Mrs. D. Allan Easton. Sire: Si-Kiang's Tashi; dam: Wei-Honey Gold of Elfann. Trari is a ten-pound gold specimen with black mask and tippings. Her breeding goes back to Swedish and French dogs on her father's side and her mother is from England. She was also the subject of the Jeffrey Dali portrait on the outside back cover of this book.

About the Authors

THE REVEREND D. ALLAN EASTON,
F.R.A.S., M.A., B.D., S.T.M.

Equally at home in Europe, Asia, or North America, the Rev.
D. Allan Easton is a Fellow of the Royal Asiatic Society of Great
Britain and Ireland and a Member of the American Oriental Society,
the China Institute of America, the Tibet Society of the United Kingdom, and the International Platform Association which unites public
speakers and writers of the free world.

Born and raised in Scotland, Mr. Easton began his travels as a
student when he signed on as purser on a British freighter for an

eight week round trip voyage to Rio de Janeiro, Montevideo, and Buenos Aires.

After completing his studies in Glasgow and New York, Mr. Easton first visited Peking in 1937, a few days before the Japanese took over the city, and thus experienced something of the fascination of pre-Pearl Harbor life in the ancient Chinese capital. From that experience he traces the beginning of his present enthusiasm for the rare little Lion Dogs from the Manchu Palace.

In 1938, while acting as Professor of Civics at an Indian college in the Himalayas, Mr. Easton became one of the few Europeans to visit the hidden land of Tibet. Made by mule and pony across a 15,000 foot mountain pass, accompanied only by a Ghurka attendant, this expedition took him to Gyantse, third largest "town" in Tibet.

Beginning with an invitation to dinner at the Royal Palace in Gangtok, where the Scottish traveller discovered that he shared a common interest in pet monkeys with the Maharajah of Sikkim, the six-week, 400 mile journey included a luncheon in a Tibetan monastery and tea parties with high ranking officials and members of the nobility.

Travelling across India some months later, by sheer chance Mr. Easton found himself sharing a railway carriage with the late Mahatma Ghandi and sleeping on the berth immediately above that of the revered Asian leader. During the twenty-four hour journey, understandably, many assumed Mr. Easton to be the Mahatma's newest Western disciple!

The Rev. Easton was invited to return to Peking in 1947. Before leaving for Hong Kong two years later, he lived through the six-week siege of the city and for seven months under the Communist regime.

Spending a year as Executive Director of the Honolulu Council of Churches, Mr. Easton organized his own weekly radio program of religious news and represented the churches of Hawaii at the 1950 Mid-Century White House Conference on Children and Youth and other important mainland conferences.

In 1951 Mr. Easton returned to Scotland. After his marriage in Ireland in 1954, he and his wife, Margaret, spent some years in an historic Scottish rural parish with ten acres of glebe or "minister's land." There they raised goats, hens, turkeys, geese and ducks in addition to having as house-pets Siamese cats, Pekingese, and Tibetan Terriers. One of these Terriers was especially treasured, having been smuggled out of its homeland by an Indian disguised as a beggar.

In 1960 Mr. Easton was called to New Jersey where he is now both Rector of St. Paul's Episcopal Church in Woodridge, and World Affairs Chairman for the Episcopal Diocese of Newark. In 1963 he was awarded a citation for "Outstanding Public Service" from the U.S. Cuban Refugee Emergency Center in Miami for his resettlement of a plane-load of 97 Cuban refugees in Northern New Jersey.

In 1964 Governor Richard J. Hughes of Trenton highly commended Mr. Easton for his visit to the quake stricken areas of Alaska on behalf of the people of New Jersey, a visit which led to the Juneau Secretary of State decorating him with the "Order of the Alaska Walrus." This six-week, 10,000 mile round trip was made together with Mrs. Easton, their two small sons, an Afghan Hound and three Shih Tzu, all of whom shared the same tent!!

In 1965 Mr. Easton's church was selected by Governor Hughes as the place of release for his official tribute to Sir Winston Churchill in which the New Jersey Governor made moving reference to the importance of Anglo-American relations. On numerous occasions Mr. Easton has represented the churches of New Jersey at important meetings in Washington, and other large cities and is a regular contributor to the church press. Trained at the Newspaper Institute of America, he has been Shih Tzu columnist for *Popular Dogs* magazine for many years.

Mr. and Mrs. Easton's first Shih Tzu was purchased in 1961 from the Pennsylvania fancier, Ingrid Colwell, and they have since imported dogs from England, Germany, and Holland, breeding selectively to produce their own outstanding Chumulari line.

A registered nurse trained in Edinburgh, Margaret Easton takes the full responsibility for the care and feeding of the Chumulari dogs and for their magnificent presentation in the show ring. Born in India of Scottish parents, she remembers camping out in the foothills of the Himalayas with the mysterious land of Tibet beyond. Ever since, dogs of oriental origin have always fascinated her.

The Easton's permanent home is now in Nova Scotia where they own a 100-year-old farmhouse and thirty acres of land by the shores of the remote and lovely Bras d'Or Lake on Cape Breton Island, their neighbors being descendants of Scottish highlanders who left their native land more than a century ago. They are members of Kennel Clubs in Nova Scotia and New Jersey, and belong to the Dog Fanciers' Club of New York.

JOAN McDONALD BREARLEY

Joan Brearley has been attracted to animals since she was old enough to know what they were.

Over the years there has been a constant succession of dogs, cats, birds, fish, rabbits, snakes, turtles, baby alligators, squirrels, lizards, etc., for her own personal menagerie. Through these same years she has owned over twenty different breeds of purebred dogs, as well as countless mixtures, since the door was never closed to a needy or homeless animal.

A graduate of the American Academy of Dramatic Arts, Joan started her career as a writer for movie magazines, and as an actress and dancer. She has also been a scriptwriter, actress, and producer-director in radio and television in New York City.

Her credits in the dog fancy include American Kennel Club approved judge, breeder-exhibitor of top show dogs, writer for the *American Kennel Gazette*, and she wrote "This Is the Afghan Hound," the breed book for these hounds of antiquity. Since August of 1967 she has been editor of *Popular Dogs*, the national prestige magazine that sets the pace for the entire dog fancy.

She is an avid crusader and speaker for humane legislation for animals. Speaking before kennel clubs on behalf of the good and welfare of all animals, she has received many awards and citations for her work in this field.

As active in the cat world as she is in the dog fancy, Joan lives in a penthouse apartment overlooking Rittenhouse Square in Philadelphia with an Afghan Hound and a dozen or more cats, most of which are Best in Show winners and are professional models for television and magazines. She has the rare distinction of having bred a Westminster Kennel Club group winner in her first litter of Afghan Hounds; Ch. Sahadi Shikari, the top-winning Afghan Hound in the history of the breed.

In addition to her activities in the dog world, Joan spends much time at the art and auction galleries, the theatre, creating needlepoint (for which she has also won awards), the opera, the typewriter —and the zoo!

Introduction

The Shih Tzu captured my fancy and imagination from the very first moment I laid eyes on one of these incomparable, adorable, shaggy mops!

When I took over as Editor of *Popular Dogs* magazine in 1967 I made it one of the first orders of business to become acquainted with The Reverend D. Allan Easton, our learned Shih Tzu columnist. His monthly commentaries on this rare breed had always been one of the first things I read when I received my issue of the magazine each month.

A lengthy correspondence developed, nurtured with pertinent telephone calls. Eagerly anticipated, but all too brief, visits at dog shows ensued, where my hands would fall upon the excellent specimens of Shih Tzu the Eastons would be presenting in the show ring with their usual charm and grace. And always with the ultimate dream of eventually receiving American Kennel Club stud book recognition for the little Lion Dogs from Peking.

As the day of recognition came closer and closer it became more and more evident that my questions and the Reverend Easton's endless dedication to researching this breed were developing into a breed book. "This Is The Shih Tzu" is that book . . .

It is the first and only comprehensive history of the Peking Tribute dogs. A book destined to become the Bible for the breed for years to come, based on personal experiences and observations in the country of their origin right up to the present day, written by the world authority on the breed . . . the man who has dedicated himself to their presentation and perfection in the modern world of dogs. The book contains all the infinite detail and research so essential to a breed book which introduces a newly accepted breed to the American public, as the Shih Tzu gained status with the American Kennel Club on September 1, 1969.

Writing this book with The Reverend Easton has been an exhilarating experience, not only because of my respect for his integrity as a person and his insatiable appetite for detail and truth, but because he has introduced me to all the joys and idiosyncrasies of yet another fascinating breed in my personal and wonderful world of dogs! For this I shall always be personally grateful . . .

I know you will be too.

Joan Brearley
Philadelphia, Pennsylvania
September, 1969

CHAPTER I

THE HISTORY OF THE SHIH TZU

Late in 1948, when I was Pastor of the Peking Union Church, an interdenominational body attended by English-speaking Protestants of many nationalities, the near approach of the Red Army made my position highly precarious.

Anxious that I should not have to desert the English-speaking community at such a critical time, the Secretary of the Peiping Chancery of the Netherlands Embassy in China, like many other western diplomats an active member of my congregation, made a generous offer which provided me with considerable security and some measure of diplomatic status.

I still treasure the official document, written in English and Chinese and bearing the Embassy seal, which certifies that I was "in the service of the Netherlands Government and as such included in the Administrative Staff of the Netherlands in China."

My responsibility was to take charge of one of the two Netherlands Embassy "compounds" in Peking, if necessary holding the Communists back at the gate on the grounds that it was diplomatic property.

For this service I received a nominal salary, free housing, light, heat, and water. Also included were the services of a watch-dog, of uncertain origin, for which the Netherlands Government granted a feeding allowance.

Since my presence on the Dutch compound was of little importance until the Red Army took over the city, to augment my finances during the six-week siege of Peking I worked by day for an American medical committee. My responsibility was to distribute supplies to the various city hospitals in order to prevent the supplies falling into the wrong hands.

In addition, at the last minute I was invited to look after the German Lutheran community, at that time left without a pastor.

For these six weeks I lived in China with a British passport, maintaining a vast variety of international contacts, driving by day in a jeep flying the Stars and Stripes, sleeping by night under the Dutch tricolor, and on the side caring for a German congregation!

Although my American post was of limited duration I remained at my Dutch one for seven months after the arrival of the Communist troops. Is it surprising that I cherish an undying love for the flag upon whose hospitable shelter I depended during the siege of Peking and for so long under the Mao Tse-tung Government? Such experiences are not readily forgotten.

LAST KNOWN SHIH TZU IN CHINA

During these difficult days, so far as I know, the only Shih Tzu bred in Peking were those of Mr. Alfred Koehn, a German, author

A view of the Tibetan plateau from an elevation of 18,000 feet. It is from this remote mountain fastness that the early ancestors of the Shih Tzu came into being. These dogs were taken from Tibet to Peking as gifts and were bred to Chinese Palace dogs to develop the exquisite Shih Tzu.

These Shih Tzu were the property of Mr. Alfred Koehn, a German author and publisher who lived in Peking during the Japanese occupation. This photograph is believed to have been taken in the late 1940's. Prevailing conditions at the time must have made selective breeding most difficult.

and publisher of many beautiful books on Chinese and Japanese arts and crafts.

At almost exactly the same time as the Communist siege of the city began, a full-page advertisement for these dogs appeared in the Christmas, 1948, issue of the British magazine *Our Dogs*, on page 21. This advertisement showed photographs of six of Mr. Koehn's Shih Tzu beside which was stated—"They are descendants of the Lion Dogs which came to China during the Manchu Dynasty as tributes from Tibet or as gifts from the Grand Lamas to the Imperial Court in Peking."

Clearly at that time it was the prevailing belief in China that the

Shih Tzu were of Tibetan origin. "Dr. C. Walter Young in his monograph on *Some Canine Breeds of Asia* mentions that there is much evidence to 'support the claim that the shock-headed variety of small dog so commonly seen in Peiping are Tibetan in origin'." This from the preface of Madame Lu's *The Lhassa Lion Dog*, originally published by the Peking Kennel Club in the mid-1930s.

From his experiences of life in the Peking palace some twenty years previously Colonel Valentine Burkhardt reached a similar conclusion. First visiting the Chinese capital in 1913, in his *Chinese Creeds and Customs* Colonel Burkhardt describes "the small dogs" which he found to be "popular" there. These are classified as the native Pekingese, the Chinese Pug, and "the Tibetan, always referred to as the 'Lion' or shih-tze kou." (Kou means Dog, Shih-Tze, or Shih Tzu, Lion.)

The same opinion regarding the Shih Tzu's origin is found in articles about the breed which appeared in the Chinese English-

The Lotus Court in the Summer Palace a few miles outside Peking. This was a favorite summer home of the Imperial Court during the last years of the Manchu Dynasty. The Empress Dowager Tzu Hsi was very partial to this spot and probably enjoyed the company of her lion dogs here as well.

18

These Shih Tzu are examples of the highly-prized golden color that was held in such high esteem by the Imperial house. They are (l. to r.) Ch. Lhakang Chin-Pao of Elfann, Sing-erh of Lhakang and Lhakang Mimosa of Northallerton.

language press at the time when it was first becoming known to the western world.

You might see, for example, the *China Journal* of Shanghai, February 1933 issue on pages 111–113, and May 1934 issue on page 298, in the New York Public Library, or the *Peiping Chronicle*, May 17th, 1936, page 7, and the *North China Star* of Tientsin, May 17th, 1937, page 14. The latter two are available in the Library of Congress in Washington, D.C.

To return to Mr. Koehn's dogs, so far as I know the last Shih Tzu of his breeding to leave Peking were taken out by a British diplomat who was a member of my congregation and who left for Hong Kong in October or November, 1948.

Owing to the strain of these revolutionary days and the time since elapsed, I have little detailed recollection of this pair of Shih Tzu, one male, one female, but they were probably golden and I am quite sure that they were small. My one certain memory is that of two little creatures gambolling together on the living room carpet and of

Mai-Ting and Wuffles with their daughter Pui-Yao. Mai-Ting, a black and white and Wuffles, a golden, were among the last Shih Tzu ever to leave China. Their names can be found in many pedigrees of the best English and American specimens of the breed.

my picking them both up together with the greatest of ease. I have since lost all trace of them.

Probably bred by Mr. Koehn about a year before the Communist take-over of Peking in January, 1949,* another Shih Tzu, "Wuffles," was acquired by a British couple in nearby Tientsin who took him home to England when they left North China by air immediately prior to the advance of the Red Army.

Described as "a most beautiful camel-colored Shih Tzu dog" with "a beautiful full coat," Wuffles was accidentally killed by an English truck in early 1952, aged only four. Fortunately he was not without issue.

One other Shih Tzu, a bitch named "Mai-Ting," came out of China in April, 1949, but she was from Shanghai and her breeder is

---

* "Peking" means "Northern Capital," the historic name of the city and that in use today. For a brief period between 1928 and 1949, when the capital was moved by the Nationalist Government to "Nanking" or "Southern Capital," the name of Peking was officially changed to "Peiping" or "Northern Peace."

In this book the names Peiping and Peking are used interchangeably, as was the popular custom from 1928 to 1949.

Jemima of Lhakang, owned by Rev. and Mrs. D. Allan Easton and bred in England under the supervision of Mrs. L. G. Widdrington. "Jigme" is a great-great-grand-daughter of Mai-Ting and is said to resemble her closely.

unknown. In the summer of 1948 Mai-Ting was produced from under the driver's seat by a Chinese chauffeur as a surprise gift for some British Consulate children whom he was in the habit of driving to school each day.

Information about the little puppy's background was not available except for the assurance that she came from the house of a "Number One Chinese family" in Shanghai. The expression "Number One" was used by Chinese servants to indicate unqualified approval. Probably they were referring to the home of a high class Chinese family who may well have been compelled to flee from the city at that time.

Obviously impressed by the value of the gift, other Chinese agreed that the black and white ball of fluff was indeed a "Number One Peking Dog." This estimate of Mai-Ting's worth was confirmed by the Consul-General and another leading British official with extensive knowledge of Tibet and China.

By special permission of the Captain, Mai-Ting was permitted to leave Shanghai in April, 1949, on the Royal Naval vessel sent to evacuate United Kingdom citizens to Hong Kong in the face of growing Communist threats—a unique honor for a dog, but no unfitting method of travel for what may well have been the last native-born representative of the royal breed to leave her homeland to spend the rest of her life in exile in far-off lands.

Shipped in more orthodox fashion from Hong Kong to England, Mai-Ting was mated to Wuffles only once, the result being a single black and white bitch, whelped in October, 1950. After spending three years of her life at the British Embassy in Cyprus, Mai-Ting died in England in August, 1962, at the ripe old age of $14\frac{1}{2}$.

Said to resemble her distinguished ancestor closely, Mai-Ting's great-great grand-daughter is an honored member of our family circle today. Known to us as Jigme, Jemima of Lhakang flew across the Atlantic in November, 1965, having been personally selected for export by Mrs. L. G. Widdrington, leading English authority on the breed. Jigme's photograph received wide-spread publicity when it appeared in the Sunday edition of the *New York Times* on January 8th, 1967.

Another bitch is reported to have been imported into England from China in 1952, but so far I have been able to trace no detailed reference to her story. Possibly she originated in Taiwan or Hong Kong, as by that time it seems unlikely that it would have been possible to take dogs out of mainland China. In this regard I may be mistaken, however, and I am still hoping for more extensive information.

These last imports from China are of particular interest since the breed must be presumed to be extinct in that country today. This presumption is strengthened by a letter, dated July 1st, 1966, written by the Honorary Secretary of the Hong Kong Kennel Club. Published in the British magazine, *Shih Tzu News*, in December of

Mrs. R. Laurenz with Mei Mei (left) and Mo'er. At the China Kennel Club show of 1930 Mo'er was the first prize winner in a class for "Tibetan Poodles." The show was held in Shanghai and marked the first occasion that Shih Tzu were shown in any numbers at a western style dog show.

the same year, this letter expresses interest in securing Shih Tzu from the West, both "pet and exhibition type," for members who apparently could not find them in Asia.

EARLIER SHIH TZU EXPORTS FROM CHINA

Of course, the Shih Tzu had reached the West some twenty-five years before the Communist Revolution, a few having been brought to Great Britain, Ireland, and to Scandinavia during the early 1930s, others following to Great Britain some years later.

The Scandinavian imports were of peculiar interest, being brought home by Mrs. Henrik Kauffman, wife of the Danish Minister to China who was later his country's Ambassador in London and Washington. Since the Kauffman's were transferred from Peking to the Danish Legation in Oslo, the three Shih Tzu were registered with the Norwegian Kennel Club, a fact ascertained from a letter written by Mr. Turid Moen, Secretary of the Norwegian Kennel Club, to Miss Astrid Jeppesen, and dated September 14th, 1965.

Ting-a-Ling (left), owned by Mrs. Else Grume and Aidzo, owned by Mrs. Henrik Kauffmann. Aidzo was one of the original imports that Mr. and Mrs. Kauffmann brought out of China with them and was one of the pillars of the Shih Tzu breed in Scandinavia.

The late Henrik Kauffmann, Ambassador of Denmark to the United States. Mr. Kauffmann and his wife, brought over some of the earlier imports from Peking. It was they who secured dogs of choice Palace breeding to establish the smaller Shih Tzu as the most sought-after type among continental fanciers.

Aidzo (left) and Leidza, owned by Mr. and Mrs. Henrik Kauffmann. This photograph was taken in Norway shortly after the arrival of these dogs from China. Both dogs were born in Peking, and leidza came directly from the Imperial Palace. The fact that these dogs were available to westerners had a great impact on the breed and influenced the whole future of the Shih Tzu all around the world.

An interesting story is attached to the Kauffman's first acquisition of a Shih Tzu. It is said that Mrs. Kauffman saw some dogs in Peking which were to be burnt, possibly in connection with a funeral ceremony although normally the burning of models made of paper or cypress twigs was regarded as sufficient to ensure that the real thing would be at the disposal of the deceased in the after-world.

Feeling sorry for the innocent victims, Mrs. Kauffman begged that their lives be spared, finally taking one home to the Danish Ministry with her. As a result she took such a liking to the breed that two others of the same type were added to her household later, one from the Imperial Palace, the other from Shanghai.

Although strange, this vivid account comes to us from Mrs. Adele Heyerdahl of Oslo who was given one of the Kauffman's first

Norwegian-born puppies and who remained an ardent Shih Tzu breeder until her death thirty years later. Since Mrs. Heyerdahl helped Mrs. Kauffman to register her imports with the Norwegian Kennel Club in 1934, her knowledge of their story seems likely to be accurate.

More prosaically, the Norwegian Kennel Club account runs—

"The names of the dogs which were imported from Peking by the wife of Minister Kauffman are: 'Aidzo' 12180, 'Leidza' 12182, and 'Schauder' 12183.

" 'Aidzo' was born in Peking in March 1930; his father was 'Law-Hu,' his mother, 'Lun-Geni.' 'Leidza' was born in the Imperial Palace in Peking in May 1928; her father was 'Chintai,' her mother, 'Wu-hi.' 'Schauder' was born in Shanghai in December 1931; her father was 'Aidzo-Huh,' her mother 'Hu-Luh'."

Since missing numbers raise questions it should be explained that NKC 12181 was 'Lingen,' a male Shih Tzu bred by the Kauffman's in Norway. Although obviously some years younger, in the process

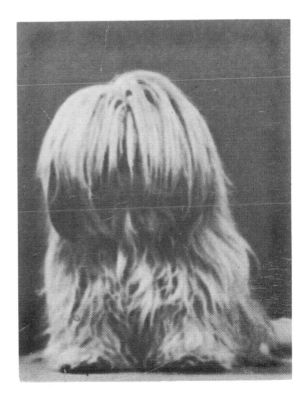

Ting-a-Ling, owned by Mrs. Else Grum and bred by Mrs. Henrik Kauffmann. Sire: Lingen, one of the first dogs bred by the Kauffmanns from their original imports; dam: Leidza, the bitch the Kauffmanns secured from the Imperial Palace in Peking. A litter brother of Ting-a-Ling, Choo-Choo, was presented as a gift to the British Royal Family.

of registration 'Lingen' was given a lower number than two of the imports from which he was descended.

Naturally quarantine restrictions would keep the Kauffmans from taking their Shih Tzu to London, but one wonders whether or not they accompanied them to the United States. We do know that a puppy of this line was presented to Queen Elizabeth, then Duchess of York, in 1933 and was later used at stud in England.

Followed later by his grandson, Ching, this dog quickly became one of the British Royal Family's favorite pets, accompanying them on their visits to their Scottish summer home and elsewhere on their travels.

"We called him Choo-Choo," King George VI once explained,

The Imperial Gate in the ancient Capital of Vietnam, Hue. Shih Tzu were also known in this and other areas adjacent to China proper.

The Royal Family relaxing with their dogs at Windsor. The Queen Mother (right) holds Choo-Choo the Shih Tzu bred by Mrs. Henrik Kauffmann.

"because when he first came to us he made noises exactly like a train!" The King would jokingly refer to Choo-Choo as "the animated dish-cloth" or "the hairy monster."

Keeping himself aloof from the five other dogs in the royal household, as though aware of his unique lineage, Choo-Choo enjoyed one very special privilege. Whenever the Queen took him up in her arms, as she frequently did, the self-assured Shih Tzu would solemnly nibble her corsage. "Without comment Princess Elizabeth would pick another sprig of jasmine, and with equal gravity Choo-Choo would chew that also—and once again only a cluster of stalks would adorn the Queen's jacket."

As might be expected, the association with royalty did much to draw favorable attention to the breed in the United Kingdom, particular notice being taken of the fact that the Shih Tzu had also enjoyed a privileged place at the Chinese Court. The breed's Tibetan ancestry created widespread interest, especially when it was reported that in Tibet dogs of this type had been trained to turn prayer wheels by those unwilling to undertake this responsibility for themselves. Such wheels, or drums, were filled with written prayers which were believed to ascend to heaven with each revolution of the container. These could be turned by dogs in the same way as dogs were used to turn cooking-spits in old England.

Since he was getting old and blind and liable to be upset by gun-fire, during World War II Choo-Choo was evacuated to the Queen's family home and birthplace which had been turned into a military hospital. A moving story is told of his reunion with his royal mistress (now the Queen Mother) when she paid a visit to the soldier invalids.

"The soldiers were gathered in the large drawing-room when the Queen came in. Choo-Choo was asleep on the hearthrug.

"Suddenly he sat up and sniffed the air. Then practically turning a somersault in his eagerness, he hurled himself across the room at the beloved mistress whom he had not seen for so many months.

"The Queen was taken off her guard. In a moment she was kneeling on the floor, with the little lion-dog throwing himself ecstatically upon her, pulling her hat and her hair in his eagerness.

"It was as if both had forgotten there were any others in the room.

"Then the Queen stood up and laughed apologetically as she

Ch. Maya Wong of Lhakang and her daughter Ch. Jou-Li of Lhakang, Jou-Li traces her ancestry back to Chinese imported stock of the Palace type.

Ch. Bjorneholms Leidza, owned by Mrs. Birgitta Sabats of Sweden and bred by Miss Astrid Jeppesen of Denmark.

picked Choo-Choo up and carried him around in her arms throughout the inspection."

An equally moving account is given of the reunion of the present Queen (then Princess Elizabeth) with the royal Shih Tzu after an enforced separation during the years of war.

While Shih Tzu fanciers take a natural pride in such stories of royal recognition, they can hardly be expected to be surprised. Somehow it seems only right that the pride of the Peking court should similarly be honored at Buckingham Palace. American fanciers may be permitted to wonder when the little aristocrats will be permitted to grace the White House with their presence.

In my opinion there are sound historical reasons for considering the Shih Tzu brought to Scandinavia as more representative specimens of the imperial lion dogs than those brought to England at the same time.

In those days the Chinese felt the British to be specially responsible for the "unequal treaties" forced on them thirty years previously that gave westerners a privileged position in China. Since they particularly resented the foreign troops stationed in their country, it seems unlikely that the Chinese would have made the best of the treasured little dogs available to the high-ranking British military officers who brought most of the first ones home to England. Indeed it may be strongly suspected that they would derive considerable satisfaction from misleading them.

For an explanation of Chinese feelings towards the British at this time we need only read *A History of the Far East in Modern Times*, by Harold Vinacke. Here it is described how the Chinese leaders "singled out England as the principal target for their propaganda against imperialism . . . The national propagandist needed concrete acts undertaken by particular states to focus attention on as evidence of imperialism . . . These were at this time supplied him by the British."

What this meant in practice is vividly described in *Chasmu Shih Tzu, International Newssheet, No. 4*, where an English traveller, Mrs. Audrey Fowler, depicts the lengths to which she was led to believe the Chinese would be prepared to go to prevent her Shih Tzu leaving the country with her.

Handing over to the care of the ship's butcher two puppies she had acquired through the Countess d'Anjou and was taking home to England, Mrs. Fowler was "horrified" to be told that they would only live for a few days. When she asked why, she was told, "The Chinese always give their puppies powdered glass just before they leave as they do not want them to leave the country." How thankful I was," Mrs. Fowler exclaims, "I had not bought them from a Chinese."

A not dissimilar account of her experiences is given by the Countess d'Anjou who, as a Frenchwoman, also came from a nation which had its troops stationed in China and enjoyed other special concessions. The Countess gives a colorful description of her difficulties in securing Shih Tzu during this period, and of the extraordinary obstacles placed in her way by the Chinese.

"At first I bought grown females and they had never had puppies," she reminisced sadly. "They had certainly done something to keep them from having them. The Lamas in the temples behind Peking also bred them but refused to sell them."

Fortunately she secured the co-operation of the Paris-educated Princess Der Ling who was in a unique position to help her, having been for two years a lady-in-waiting to the Empress Dowager.

I was particularly interested to discover the evidence regarding the Princess' French schooling in the *China Weekly Chronicle*, dated October 13th, 1935, on page 22. The Countess' account of her difficulties in securing Shih Tzu, and of the help given to her by the Princess, will be found in her *Description of the Shih Tzu* written in Peking in 1938 and published in England in the booklet *Chasmu Shih Tzu*, edited by Mrs. Fowler, though no date is given.

No such Chinese ill-feeling placed difficulties in the way of the Danish diplomat and his wife, since they were in a wholly different situation. They represented a small country which had no troops stationed on Chinese soil and which in 1928 had expressed readiness to accept the abolition of the privileged status of westerners in China. Under such circumstances it seems reasonable to suggest that the Chinese were far more likely to make the best dogs available to them.

Ch. Tien Memsahib, owned by Mrs. L. G. Widdrington and bred by Mrs. T. E. Morgan. This ten-pound, black and white was the first of the smaller type to become a Champion in England.

Ch. Chumulari Ying-Ying, owned by Rev. and Mrs. D. Allan Easton and bred by Mrs. Erika Geusendam of West Germany. Ying's dam was imported in whelp, and he was born soon after his dam's arrival here. A Canadian Champion, his record includes 3 group firsts (In Canada the Shih Tzu is classified in the Non-Sporting group), nine seconds, six thirds, nine fourths and 37 Bests of Breed. He is also the first dog of the breed to have a Best in Show win in the United States. His American record also includes five Group firsts, and he finished his championship with all major wins in less than a month from the day of breed recognition.

There is an interesting piece of evidence to substantiate this suggestion. As early as 1927 we know that a British General and his wife discovered that Shih Tzu in Peking "were not easy to find and some were very large." This was reported in the U.S. magazine, *Shih Tzu News*, Christmas, 1966, issue. Aware that "the few surviving palace Eunuchs were supposed to have some," but apparently never being permitted to see any of them, the English couple finally secured one of their two dogs from a French doctor who was returning home.

I have not been able to find any reference to the source from which the other dog was acquired, but there is nothing to suggest that either of them came from the palace, a fact which would hardly have been overlooked when their story subsequently came to be written. What is stressed is that the two Shih Tzu were secured only with difficulty and after the most painstaking study of specimens found with White Russian, French, and other breeders of unspecified nationality in Peking.

For those readers wishing to delve further into this aspect, see the English magazine, *Dog World*, of September 25th, 1959, page 1751, an article also reproduced in condensed form in the American *Dog World* magazine of November, 1967, page 111, and in the American *Shih Tzu News* magazine, December, 1966, on page 12.

A very few years later the Danish diplomat and his wife secured two small Peking-born Shih Tzu, one of them, named Leidza and subsequently bearing the Norwegian Kennel Club No. 12182, being the only known palace-born Shih Tzu to reach the West.

Leidza was born in the Peking Palace in May, 1928, thus proving conclusively that breeding was still continuing there at the time when the British couple were having such great difficulty in finding good Shih Tzu anywhere in the city. Proof of Leidza's place and date of birth is to be found in the afore-mentioned letter to Miss Jeppesen from Mr. Turid Moen, Secretary of the Norwegian Kennel Club.

Leidza's great-great-great grandson is in our possession today, inheriting the magnificent coat which the early Scandinavian imports have bequeathed to so many of their descendants. Bred for us in Germany, Chumulari Ying-Ying won his Canadian Championship in August, 1967, and—although whelped only in late January 1966—has already made a big name for himself in our adopted homeland.

In the direct line from Leidza like her son, Ch. Ying-Ying's mother, Ch. Tangra v. Tschomo-Lungma, is also in our possession

Ch. Tangra V. Tschomo-Lungma, owned by Rev. and Mrs. D. Allan Easton and bred in West Germany by Mrs. Erika Geusendam. This exquisite gold and white bitch holds the title of Champion in Switzerland, Czechoslovakia and Canada. She was declared "World Winner" by Madame Nizet de Leemans at Brno FCI World Show in 1965.

now. Retired from the show ring, she is making a highly successful debut in obedience training. Tangra came to us on the personal recommendation of Miss Astrid Jeppesen of Denmark, leading European authority on the Shih Tzu.

A Swiss, Czechoslovakian, and Canadian Champion, Tangra had already become famous before leaving Europe, having been awarded the title "World Winner" at the 1965 Brno Show in Czechoslovakia, the largest World Show arranged by the *Federation Cynologique Internationale* (a Brussels-based international organization uniting the different national kennel clubs in continental Europe) since World War II and the first major one behind the Iron Curtain.

Importing Tangra in whelp, I wrote—"Now thousands of miles from her lovely ancestral home (in Peking) Ch. Tangra brings with her a royal heritage, full of international overtones, romantic, exciting and mysterious, tragic in the light of recent events, but not without hope as she helps to introduce her breed to the new world across the seas."

Great-great-great grand-daughter of the palace-born Leidza, Tangra crossed the Atlantic in early 1966, her son Chumulari Ying-Ying being born some weeks after her arrival.

Sometimes I like to picture the scene in the Peking Palace some forty years ago as the surviving eunuchs tried to breed the finest lion dogs possible while their accustomed way of life ebbed to its close. When they gave their treasured Leidza to the distinguished visitors from far-off Denmark, did they fully understand that she would be taken away for such a distance to make her home in a strange land and among strange people? How proud they would be could they see her descendants today, most especially the gorgeous Ch. Chumulari Ying-Ying as he brings to the North American show ring so much of the charm and dignity of imperial China.

THE LAST DAYS OF PALACE BREEDING

Some charming accounts of the palace dogs are given by Miss Katharine Carl, an American artist commissioned to paint the Empress Dowager's portrait in 1903, said to be the first westerner to stay at the Peking court.

Very moving is her account of her discovery one day of a number of small tombstones, "in a beautiful shady corner, near the stables," marking the last resting places of the favorite dogs and horses of one of the Imperial Princes. "Each stone had an inscription with a name, and extolled the virtues of the favorite whose bones lay beneath it."

"The dogs at the Palace are kept in a beautiful pavilion with marble floors," Miss Carl writes. "They have silken cushions to sleep on, and special eunuchs to attend them. They are taken for daily outdoor exercise and given their baths with regularity."

According to the American artist, a very close relationship existed between the royal mistress and her dogs which were kept apart from all others. They all obeyed her implicitly, while she herself was possessive towards them in a very human way.

"The day we first met the dogs in the garden was the first time I had seen them," Miss Carl continues, "They rushed up to Her Majesty, not paying the slightest attention to anyone else. She patted their heads and caressed and spoke to her favorites. After a while they seemed to notice that a stranger was present, and they bounded over toward me. . . . I bent down to caress them, and forgot my surroundings in my pleasure at seeing and fondling these beautiful creatures.

"I glanced up, presently, never dreaming Her Majesty had been paying any attention to me, as I was standing at a little distance behind her, and I saw on her face the first sign of displeasure I had noticed there. It seems her dogs never noticed anyone but herself, and·she appeared not to like her pets being so friendly with a stranger at first sight.

"Noticing this, I immediately ceased fondling them, and they were presently sent away. It was but a momentary shadow that passed over her face, and I quite understand the feeling. One does not like to see one's pets too friendly with strangers, and I had been tactless in trying to make friends with them at once.

"A few days later, on another of our walks, some young puppies were brought to be shown the Empress Dowager. She caressed the mother and examined critically the points of the puppies. Then she called me up to show them to me, asking which I liked best. I tried not to evince too much interest in them this time, but she called my attention to their fine points and insisted upon my taking each of them up. She seemed to be ashamed of her slight displeasure of the day before, and to wish to compensate for it."

Later a eunuch brought a little dog to Miss Carl, placing it in her arms and saying that Her Majesty had ordered that it should be presented to her from the royal kennel. The Empress told Miss Carl to call the dog "Me-lah" (Golden Amber) from the color of his spots.

"Her Majesty and the Princesses were all much amused at the way he followed me around, not leaving my side for an instant, nor paying any attention to their frequent efforts to attract his attention," Miss Carl recounts proudly, "From that day, he became my constant companion and faithful friend."

Oddly enough, the Empress Dowager had a strong dislike for cats. Although some of the eunuchs had some very fine specimens, they had to be kept carefully out of sight of the royal eyes!

From various sources we get fascinating glimpses of life in the Peking Palace following the 1912 revolution and until some years after the deposed eighteen-year-old Emperor, Hsuan T'ung, finally left it in 1924.

In *Twilight in the Forbidden City*, by Sir Reginald Johnston, K.C.M.G., C.B.E., Hon. LL.D., one time tutor to the boy-Emperor and later Professor of Chinese History at the University of London, there is a detailed account of the abdication settlement drawn up in 1912 between the new Republic of China and the six-year-old Emperor. The latter was allowed to remain in the palace, occupying the throne but stripped of all political power, and was also permitted to retain "the services of all the persons of various grades hitherto employed in the Palace . . . but in future no eunuchs are to be added to the staff."

According to Miss Carl, the Empress Dowager had "Some magnificent specimens of Pekingese pugs and of a sort of Sky Terrier." We may be sure that the "sort of Skye Terriers" were Shih Tzu, particularly when we remember that Skyes were considerably smaller in those days.

"The Empress Dowager has dozens of these pets," Miss Carl continues, "but she has favorites among them, and two are privileged

Mimose (gold) and Min Yuenne (black and white), two examples of the smaller type of Shih Tzu. Both of these have the distinctive Chinese appearance about them.

characters. One of these is of the Skye variety, and is most intelligent and clever at tricks. Among other tricks, he will lie as dead at Her Majesty's command, and never move until she tells him to, no matter how many others may speak to him.

"Her other favorite she loves for his beauty. He is a splendid fawn-colored Pekingese pug, with large, pale-brown, liquid eyes. He is devoted to her, and she is very fond of him, but as he was not easily taught, even as a puppy, she called him 'Shadza,' (fool)."

The puppy given to Miss Carl is described as "a Pekingese pug," so it was not a Shih Tzu. Does this mean that the latter were too precious to be given away? If so, it would bear out the contention of Mr. Pinkham who is emphatic that he frequently heard the Princess Der Ling say that the shaggy little Shih Tzu Kou were the most treasured of the royal dogs.

Describing court life eight years later, as the princes and attendant eunuchs desperately strove to maintain a semblance of the old regime, a sympathetic observer, Juliet Bredon, calls it a "make-believe kingdom, curious and infinitely pathetic, too, this last stronghold of mystery in once mysterious Peking!"

Shih Tzu and other palace dogs continued to be bred during this twilight period, we are told, but the imperial eunuchs were largely left to their own devices as—unlike the old Empress Dowager—their lonely young master was not greatly interested. He is said to have abhorred the court pets on account of "the mess they made," and to have been only too happy to give them away to anyone. Under such circumstances mating of the royal dogs was "rather haphazard."

In these early days, we are told, a Shih Tzu came into the possession of a British Military Attache at a time when dogs were excluded from the Legation for fear of rabies. An exception was quickly made in this case, however, the little dog being officially classified as a cat!

An Italian diplomat, Daniele Vare, paints an amusing picture of his visit to the Forbidden City, as the Imperial Palace was called, on the day after it first became open to the public. Accompanied by their Fox Terrier, Tricksy, he and his Scottish-born wife joined a large number of Chinese in strolling around and "gaping" at precincts which previously had been the jealously guarded preserve of the privileged few.

"Some eunuchs watched us from the adjoining pavilions," Vare writes. "The fact that the 'stupid people' can now penetrate into the

Ch. Chumulari Ying Ying (left) and his nine-month-old daughter, Canadian Champion Carrimount Tai-Tai Chumulari. The measure of a great dog is not only expressed in his show record, but also in the quality of his progeny. This photo shows how well Ying stamps his own excellent type on his progeny.

courts of the palace must seem to them a sign of impending doom. One of the eunuchs had a little dog with him, a Pekingese. It seemed pleased to see Tricksy even though she does belong to a foreign-devil."

The Italian writer adds thoughtfully that he supposes his Fox Terrier, brought with him from Europe, to have been the first Western dog ever to have smelt the smells of the Forbidden City!

Although thoroughly familiar with life in Peking in 1912 and for some years after, it is interesting to note that Vare makes no mention

41

of the little Shih Tzu Kou with their Tibetan history. Were they still kept very much in the background, being the most precious of the Imperial Lion Dogs? To this we may never known the answer and it seems likely to remain an open question, although I have not yet heard any alternative explanation of the fact that they appear to have been so late in becoming known to the western world.

Up until 1923 there are said to have been well over 1000 eunuchs employed in the palace, but in that year most were summarily dismissed. This was due to a disastrous fire for which the eunuchs were believed to have been responsible in order to cover their large-scale theft of palace treasures.

Only about fifty were allowed to stay because the three remaining dowager consorts, "when they learned that their indispensable and more or less faithful eunuchs would no longer be there to anticipate every want and obey their lightest whispers, were filled with woe and dismay." Many more were probably allowed to return later, especially the old and crippled who knew no other home.

One of the dowagers died in the palace not long after and the remaining two were turned out on November 21st, 1924, some days before the flight of the young Emperor to Tientsin. A number of eunuchs must have remained, however, doubtless having nowhere else to go, and Lion Dog breeding clearly continued in some measure for several years. Regarding this I have been able to get little information, apart from the fact that Leidza was whelped in the Peking Palace in May, 1928—and that in itself is a not unimportant milestone in the history of the breed.

Representing another small nation which had taken a lead in the move to abolish the privileged status of westerners in China so bitterly resented by the Chinese, Monsieur Graeffe, Belgian Ambassador in Peking in the 1930s, is said to have been able to acquire six Shih Tzu descended from a pair bred in the palace in the 1920s, by name Lize and Kwanine.

Monsieur Graeffe was transferred to Iran and took his Shih Tzu with him to the Belgian Embassy in Teheran where, in 1940, he gave four puppies to Mrs. Sheila Bode, all males. One of these puppies was run over by a car in Teheran, another died of pneumonia at an early age. The two survivors lived much longer, one dying under an operation in Paris in 1949 or 1950, the other of a heart attack in Brussels in 1954.

Presumably because of quarantine difficulties, none of these dogs accompanied Mrs. Bode when she returned to England in 1944 or 1945 to become an ardent fancier of the smaller type of Shih Tzu and a founder of the *Manchu Shih Tzu Society*.

[I have since learned from Mrs. Bode, who now lives in Spain, that these four puppies were the offspring of her Pekingese bitch bred to one of M. Graeffe's Shih Tzu. This step was taken because the Belgian Ambassador's only bitch had died of distemper and there was no other Shih Tzu bitch available in wartime Teheran.

The four male puppies resulting, Mrs. Bode writes, "when adult resembled their father—the only Peke points being a somewhat shorter nose and diminutive size. They had the profuse Shih Tzu coats and temperament."

When Mrs. Bode had to return to England suddenly in 1944, owing to her husband's illness, she left the two surviving dogs with Madame Graeffe who took them to Europe after the end of the war, "when dogs were allowed to travel." One was given to a friend of

Four pioneers at the Cheltenham show in 1933 with some of the first imports into Britain. They are (l. to r.) Lady Brownrigg with Hibou, Yangtse and Shu-Ssa, Miss Hutchins of Ireland with Lung-Fu-Ssu and Tang, General Sir Douglas Brownrigg with Hzu-Hsi and Miss Wild with an Apso. In those early days Shih Tzu were still described as "Apsos."

Madame Graeffe's in Paris, the other to a friend in Switzerland. This explains the fate of the line of Shih Tzu brought out of Peking by M. Graeffe.]

THE FIRST IMPORTS TO THE BRITISH ISLES

In expressing the opinion that the Scandinavian imports were nearer to the direct imperial line, I cannot emphasize too strongly that I am in no sense criticising those who brought the first Shih Tzu to the British Isles at approximately the same time. Unquestionably these early English and Irish fanciers acted in accordance with the best knowledge available to them and went to very great trouble to secure the finest possible specimens of the breed. It was most certainly no fault of theirs if it be true that political circumstances closed for them doors which were readily opened to the Danish couple—as is clearly suggested by the fact that the latter alone were able to bring home a palace-born Shih Tzu.

Lung-Fu-Ssu (begging) and a friend. Lung-Fu-Ssu was one of the first three Shih Tzu to have been brought to Europe from Peking. Miss Hutchins brought the black and white dog to Ireland in 1930 and exhibited him at the Cheltenham show in 1933.

This photograph, taken in England in 1937, shows some of Lady Brownrigg's first Shih Tzu. They are (l. to r.) Hibou, Yangtse, Tzu-Hsi and Shu-Ssa. Hibou and Shu-Ssa were both imported and Yangtse was born in quarantine out of the latter sired by the former. Tzu-Hsi was born afterward.

An interesting photograph of these pioneers from England and Ireland, with their dogs as they appeared at the Cheltenham Show in 1933, is to be found in Hutchison's *"Popular and Illustrated Dog Encyclopaedia," Volume II*, page 1137. At that time the Shih Tzu were mistakenly described as Apsos in England, the distinction between the two breeds not being made until the following year.

Lack of detail in the photograph makes it impossible to get an altogether clear picture of the dogs, but they would appear to be delightfully characteristic "shaggy mops" and it is small wonder that they seem to have made a highly favorable impression. Of the six Shih Tzu portrayed four show distinctly bowed fore-legs, a feature which would seem to distinguish them from those in the Scandinavian line. Although not identified in the caption, standing behind the dogs are the importers, General Sir Douglas and Lady Brownrigg of England and Miss E. M. Hutchins of Ireland.

In the same volume other similarly attractive photographs of these first Shih Tzu in the British Isles appear on pages 1134, 1143, and 1146. In one instance, as in an early photograph of the Scandinavian imports, a Shih Tzu is sitting up on its hindquarters in that fascinating pose which comes so naturally to the breed and which they must have inherited from their palace ancestors.

In their *Pekingese Scrapbook*, Elsa and Ellic Howe refer to this in the chapter headed *The Princess Der Ling at the Royal Kennels*. Here the Princess is quoted as describing how, on command from the eunuch in charge, "all the dogs sat on their haunches and waited . . . Of course, some of them were awkward and had to keep trying, and the eunuch waited until all were erect, when he spoke sharply again: 'Ga Leo Fo Yea, bai bai!' which meant something like 'give greetings to Her Majesty, the Old Buddha!' The dogs barked and waved their front feet as though waving them at Her Majesty."

In the British *Kennel Gazette* of March, 1934, an illuminating

Ch. Shebo Tsemo of Lhakang, owned by Mrs. Sheila Bode and bred by Mrs. L. G. Widdrington. This grey, brown and white male was one of the larger type. He was born in 1948 and was a great-grandson of the Royal Family's Choo-Choo. One eighth of this dog's ancestry was Scandinavian, the rest was English.

Chumulari Hsing Yun, a gold bitch with black mask. She is pictured at one year of age, owner Mrs. Sandra Lucchina.

glimpse is given of the problem confronting judges in England at the time when it was gradually coming to be realized that the Shih Tzu was not the same as the Apso and should be judged separately.

Reporting on his experiences with the "Apsos, Tibetan Terriers and Spaniels" at Crufts, 1934, Mr. G. Hayes writes—"One white dog which took my fancy in the ring very much at first glance, I could not place on examination. The round eye, domed head and flat face, also the tail, made it of different type altogether, the outlook being nearer to that of the Japanese Spaniel or Pekingese. Though I did not know this at the time I ascertained afterward this dog had been bred from a dog and bitch imported from China."

Later that year it was ruled by the Tibetan Breeds Association that the dogs from China were not Apsos. After consultation with Mr. Croxton Smith, then Chairman of the Kennel Club, the name

Shih Tzu was selected for them. The sponsoring body for the separate breed was first called the Shih Tzu (Tibetan Lion Dog) Club, but in 1935 the name was shortened to the Shih Tzu Club.

At a meeting of the General Committee of the British Kennel Club on May 1st, 1934, it had already been decided that "dogs might be registered under the heading of Any Other Variety, Shih Tzu, and that those now registered as Apso could be altered without charge." Six years later, at a meeting held on May 7th, 1940, a separate register was granted to the breed which was then placed on the official list of breeds and made eligible for championship certificates.

In those early days, we are told, the appearance of the new breed aroused much interest and curiosity, newspaper reporters and photographers surrounding them whenever they were shown. First to judge a Shih Tzu in the British Isles was Mr. Jimmy Garrow who officiated at the Scottish show where the breed made its debut. Remembering the size and type of the original imports, to the end of his life Mr. Garrow put them up over the larger offspring which were soon to become increasingly evident on the British scene.

Two other especially note-worthy Shih Tzu were brought home in 1937 by an Englishwoman who visited Peking briefly in the course of an extensive world tour. Both bitches, this pair were undoubtedly small in size. The English *Our Dogs* in the Christmas, 1961, issue carried an advertisement which stressed that their "weight, when fully grown," was 12 pounds. So far as I have yet been able to discover, this is one of the clearest pieces of documentary evidence we have regarding the weight of the early Shih Tzu imports to the British Isles.

Although one appears to have been bred by Miss Frances Bieber, an American expert on Chinese folklore and on the sacred lion of Buddha, both these little Shih Tzu evidently came from the Countess d'Anjou's stock. They are described as being respectively "golden and white," and "honey" in color.

A photograph of the two puppies on board the liner, *Empress of Britain*, en route to England via Canada and the United States, suggests that both were liberally marked with white. This advertisement in the English *Dog World Annual* of December, 1962, page 31, states that the two were "purchased in Peking for the Countess d'Anjou," the word "for" presumably being a printer's slip in place

Two typical Chumulari puppies pose against an appropriately Chinese backdrop. The gold puppy (left) is three months old; the gold and white is aged four months.

of "from." In any event the Peking Kennel Club registration certificates indicate that the dam of one was owned by the Countess, the dam of the other by Miss Bieber.

Since the Countess d'Anjou was assisted by the Princess Der Ling in the selection of her stock, enabling her to overcome the obstacles placed in the way of other western fanciers by the Chinese, we may be quite sure that these two little bitches were worthy representatives of the imperial Shih Tzu at its very best. That neither of them ever had any puppies must be a matter of deep regret to all western lovers of the breed.

Although I have not yet been able to trace the reference, I am reliably informed that a Peking newspaper—almost certainly the English language *Peiping Chronicle*—carried a glowing account of the excitement which these two little Shih Tzu aroused when they were first seen in England.

Zizi's Chu-Ko-Liang, owned by Mrs. Sonja Bai and bred by Mrs. Ruth Laasko. This dog is Norwegian bred and owned. Sire: Finnish and Norwegian Ch. Marinas Muff-Lung-Feng; dam Scandinavian Ch. Zizi's Lhamo.

According to the information I have received, and I have every reason to believe it to be accurate, under the heading, *Today's Lions*, the report ran—

"The Lhassa [sic] Lion or 'Shih Tzu' is a breed very little known in Europe and America. They have been shown in London and New York for the last few years and have created a great deal of interest. Countess d'Anjou has been breeding these dogs in Peking for the last three years and has had quite a success with them. Two of her dogs were taken to England last year by Mrs. Fowler of Yew Tree

House, Winchelsea, Sussex, and shown at Crufts Dog Show in February (1938).

"Mrs. Fowler writes that they created quite a sensation. *The other dogs shown in London were much larger* and mostly black and white— very few of the honey-colored ones. It is interesting to know that the certificates issued by the Peking Kennel Club were accepted at Crufts and that *the Lhassa Lions bred here* [*in Peking*] *more than held their own with those bred in England.*"

The emphasis and the bracketed explanations by the authors.

Presumably based on information sent by the English importer in a letter to some one in Peking, the article is said to have been accompanied by two photographs. One showed the Countess with a pale-colored Shih Tzu in one hand and a cup in the other, smiling gaily; the other two heavily coated Shih Tzu, apparently light in color with dark ear-tips.

These were not the two bitches brought to England, we understand, but others belonging to the Countess in Peking. To illustrate the article the Chinese newspaper obviously had to use whatever

Gun-Yiang of Lunghwa, owned by Mrs. L. G. Widdrington and bred by Mr. and Mrs. R. Morris. This lovely black and white is a grand-daughter of Wuffles and Mai-Ting, and is the grandmother in turn of the well-known Jemima of Lhakang, owned by Rev. and Mrs. Easton.

Her Majesty the Empress Dowager Tzu Hsi and the Princess Der Ling her first lady-in-waiting. From available records it would appear that the Empress was a keen dog fancier and very partial to the Imperial Shih Tzu. It was the Princess Der Ling who, because of her close association with her Majesty, made possible the acquisition of palace stock for the breeding efforts of the Countess D'Anjou.

photographs it had on file. We have not yet seen them ourselves, but we eagerly look forward to finding them among the other fascinating material still hidden on microfilm in the library.

As has been already suggested, in our opinion the clue to the whole situation lies in the fact that the Princess Der Ling was a graduate of the Sacred Heart School in Paris, her father having represented the old Chinese Empire in several different western countries. Further details will be found in the *China Weekly Chronicle*, October 13th, 1935, and the whole story makes fascinating reading, most especially when we are told that the opportunity of entering Vassar College in the United States appealed to the young princess more strongly than that of becoming one of the ladies-in-waiting to the Empress Dowager. In spite of her familiarity with European ways, in this regard she was over-ruled by her father who counselled her to accept without question the commands of the Empress.

Wholly unique for one who was later to become an important attendant at the Manchu Court, this educational background explains the close friendship which appears to have sprung up between the Princess and the Countess d'Anjou. They must have had much

Tul-Tzu of Wyndtoi (center) and two of his daughters. These three English dogs are of the smaller type and are the property of Mrs. Roberts.

in common, not least being a shared love for the French capital. This friendship, in turn, opened doors for the Countess which had previously been closed to her, secured answers to questions which had hitherto been politely evaded, and made it possible for her to overcome the difficulties placed in her path as she strove to obtain the best possible breeding stock.

The Countess could have selected no better advisor, for the Princess has made it clear that her knowledge of the royal dogs was derived from the mouth of the Empress Dowager herself. Describing how she was first introduced to the personal pets of the old ruler, the former lady-in-waiting explains, "we went around the Ten Thousand Years Hill to the kennels, which were near the terrace where silk was dried in the sun, and on the way the Empress Dowager told me something about the dogs we were to see."

Apparently the dogs were very well trained by the attendant eunuchs and were "plainly very happy to see Her Majesty," a fact which naturally delighted the old lady. What appears to have struck

Swedish and Norwegian Champion Ta'Hay's Chwang owned and bred by Mr. Caj Rindmo of Sweden. At the age of only two years this dog has already taken two firsts in the group.

Mr. and Mrs. Edward Pinkham with their Chumulari Kung Chu. Mr. Pinkham was an avid follower of the Princess Der Ling during her American lecture tour in the 1920's. He waited patiently for almost forty years to secure one of the little lion dogs the Princess spoke of so frequently in her lectures.

the young Princess most were the intelligent eyes, fixed on their Royal Mistress. "One could not see all of the eyes, because of the long hair, but when the sun shone on them they were like tiny lights peering through the darkness."

As a footnote it should be added that the Countess died in 1965 at her daughter's home in Canada. Details of her demise were reported in the British, *Shih Tzu News*, February, 1966, on page 1, and I myself paid tribute to her memory in the American, *Popular Dogs*, of May, 1966, and in the British *Manchu Shih Tzu Society Newsletter* in June of the same year.

Much more recently I received a letter from a California Shih Tzu fancier, Mr. Stan Goldberg, dated September 19th, 1968, stating

Netherlands and International Ch. Lou Shu v.d. Oranje Manege (left), owned by Miss Aline Boudreaux and bred by Miss Eta Pauptit of the Netherlands and Chumulari Hoo T'ee owned by Anthony Mascarella and bred by Rev. and Mrs. D. Allan Easton. Both dogs reside in Dhahran, Saudi Arabia where their owners are in the service of the Arabian-American Oil Company.

that the Princess, who was teaching at the University of California, had been hit by a car and killed "several years ago." Not a little pathetically, the letter adds that the press report of the accident was "very small in a world that had long forgotten her and the grandeur of the court of China."

As I have discovered even more recently, however, the Princess is by no means wholly forgotten. Among those who remember her with gratitude and affection is Mr. Ed Pinkham, Shih Tzu fancier of Rhode Island, who tells me that he followed her eagerly when she lectured in New England some forty years ago. Although it was a long time ago, Mr. Pinkham insists that he clearly recalls the Princess Der Ling emphasizing more than once that the little Tibetan Shih Tzu Kou were the most precious of all the royal dogs. If this be so, we can be confident that she made sure that the best possible specimens were made available to her French friend when she returned to Peking after her lecture tour.

Acquired from the Countess d'Anjou in 1937, the two 12 pound bitches which took London by storm in the following year must probably be classed among the finest specimens of the breed to have reached the shores of the United Kingdom by that time. In the light of their background in Peking and their link with the Princess they may well have fallen very little short of equalling in quality that brought home to Scandinavia from the palace by Mrs. Henrik Kauffman a few years earlier and it is by no means inconceivable that they were of similar high caliber.

Unfortunately the unique little pair died without leaving issue. The importer, Mrs. Fowler, has written that she was too occupied to think of breeding puppies, owing to the outbreak of war in 1939, and "then one was run over by an army lorry (truck) and the other too precious to mate." Had they only left descendants by a carefully selected sire of similar, or preferably of smaller size, assuming such to have been available in England at the time, this pair of 12 pound bitches might well have exercised a decisive influence on the whole subsequent course of Shih Tzu history in the United Kingdom and beyond.

In a letter written to me, dated January 7th, 1966, Mrs. Fowler, the importer of the two Shih Tzu concerned, wrote—"These I brought back, when they came out of quarantine weighed 14–16 lbs. respectively." Obviously this is a slip of memory, as evidenced by the emphatic statement in the Christmas issue of the English magazine, *Our Dogs*, five years earlier, below the photograph of the two Shih Tzu, "weight when fully grown, 12 lbs."

While the mistake is understandable it does illustrate sharply that the unaided human memory is subject to error after the lapse of nearly thirty years. While great experiences stick in our minds, details become blurred astonishingly quickly. Since undocumented recollections can lead to confusion regarding figures and dates, in such matters it is wise to rely only on such written evidence as is available.

CHAPTER II

COLOR AND APPEARANCE

Present-day standards prescribe no fixed color for the Shih Tzu, a position which may be explained by the varieties of coloring which have been seen in the breed since it first became known to the western world.

Interestingly enough, the first and second prize-winners at the Shanghai Kennel Club Show of May 30th, 1930, probably among the first Shih Tzu ever to appear in a western-style show ring, were all black in color. Their photographs are to be seen in two consecutive issues of the *China Journal*, those of June and August, 1930.

Black and white was also frequently in evidence, so much so that the Countess d'Anjou somewhat disparagingly described them as "striking," but "very ordinary and not as precious as the golden." She made this observation in a letter to Mrs. L. G. Widdrington from Juan-Les-Pins in France, dated May, 1955, which was reprinted in the American *Shih Tzu News*, March, 1967.

At the court golden-yellow, sometimes described as honey, was the "favorite" or "proper" color, and it has been claimed that these were the only ones kept in the palace. There may a measure of truth in this, but it is not clearly stated in the Countess' letter and Elsa and Ellis Howe assert that three of the Empress Dowager's "sleeve dogs" were greyish-white. We may be reasonably sure that these were not Shih Tzu Kou, however, as the "Tibetans" normally did not quite fit into the "sleeve" category, or so we are led to believe by Colonel Valentine Burkhardt.

Fuller details regarding Chinese views on color will be found in *The Lhassa Lion Dog* by Madame Lu who makes the interesting point that "the yellow color of Lhassa Lion Dogs is more like that of a camel. If it is a bright and glossy yellow, the dog is not of a pure breed type."

Si-Kiang's Tashi, owned by Rev. and Mrs. D. Allan Easton and bred by the late Ingrid Colwell. Tashi, a solid-black, American-bred male is another of the smaller type with a weight of ten pounds. He was Best in Match at the first Shih Tzu fun match held in the U.S.A. This match drew an entry of over forty with dogs coming from all over the east and from as far west as the state of Colorado.

In the Imperial Court Shih Tzu of the golden color were considered to be the most desirable. This was because the color of these dogs most closely approximated that of the lion. In the great majority of cases the dogs seen outside the palace walls were not of this highly-prized golden hue.

Yellow was the imperial color, of course, a fact not easily forgotten by anyone who has seen the golden-yellow tiled roofs of the Peking Palace. Yellow dogs are also more lion-like in appearance and it, must not be overlooked that the word "Shih Tzu" means "Lion" in Chinese, the little dogs having been bred to resemble that animal as the Chinese conceived it. Although it is highly unlikely that many of them had ever seen a real one, the lion not being indigenous to China, they had a long-standing familiarity with "the fancy conventionalized types of lions introduced into China from India with Buddhism." The quotation is from Berthold Laufer's *Chinese Pottery of The Han Dynasty* which describes in detail how the lion motif made an enduring impression in old China as "its numerous

Although it is highly unlikely that most Chinese living during the Manchu Dynasty had ever seen a lion in the flesh there were still many popular conceptions of the lion in Chinese art. This interesting photograph shows a comparison between two carved ivory Chinese lion dogs and a modern Shih Tzu puppy seven weeks of age.

connections with the legends woven around Buddha and the saints deeply appealed to the popular mind."

Faced with the existence by that time of a variety of colors but anxious to do justice to the facts of history, the 1938 Peking Kennel Club standard for the Shih Tzu runs, "all colors permissible, single and mixed. Tawny or honey-coloured highly favoured."

From this the 1958 British standard selects only, "all colors permissible," but adds the words, "a white blaze on the forehead and a white tip to the tail are highly prized." Also permitting any color, the French standard of the mid-1950s comments "honey-colored and white are rare and much appreciated."

The mention of white in the latter standard reflects the fact that a leading French breeder in Peking—not the Countess d'Anjou—had a large number of all-white Shih Tzu, but it must be questioned

Ch. Chumulari Li-Tzu, owned by Mrs. Marilyn M. Guiraud, is a gold and white bitch with black tippings. Li-Tzu also caries the highly desirable white blaze and tail tip. This has been described as giving the Shih Tzu the appearance of a boat in full sail when the dog is moving.

Jemima of Lhakang, owned by Rev. and Mrs. D. Allan Easton is typical of the black and white coloring so often seen in the Shi Tzu. These were among the first that were available to western fanciers, and this would account for their early prevalence at many shows that were held outside China.

whether the "appreciation" shown for them did not come more from westerners than from natives of the city. Some six hundred years previously it is true that the Mongol, or Yuan, Dynasty did not share Chinese feelings on the subject, according to V. W. F. Collier's *Dogs of China and Japan in Nature and Art*, but in general there seems little doubt that "a pure white dog, being the color of mourning, was not an asset, as the Chinese hate to be reminded of death."

Apparently this aversion did not apply to white markings in the appropriate places which were highly prized. The fullest reference

Canadian Ch. Chumulari Sheng-Li Che, owned and bred by Rev. and Mrs. D. Allan Easton. Sire: Ch. Chumulari Ying-Ying; dam: Chumulari Trari. This gold and white homebred is pictured at seven months.

to them in modern standards, although lacking in detail, appears to be in the "Breed Classification" for the Shih Tzu, handed by the American Kennel Club to judges while judging them in the Miscellaneous Class, which ran "all colors are allowable but in general the darker shades predominate. The white blaze, collar, socks and tail-tip combine to create a highly prized ensemble."

Since the Chinese regarded the yellow-colored Shih Tzu as especially precious it is understandable that it should have been particularly hard for westerners to lay hands on them, the Countess d'Anjou being very greatly privileged in this regard for the reason already stated. We are told, in *The Lion Dog Through the Looking*

Many breeds of dogs are said to reflect their national origins in their facial expressions. This is especially so in the case of the Shih Tzu. He looks every inch the Manchu aristocrat, and those that are closest to him say that he conducts himself as though he knows it.

Glass, that it was the black and white, and grey and white, which first were found on the market at street fairs in China, and even in their case exportation was at first forbidden.

When it did become possible to export specimens of the breed, not unnaturally it would appear that the least favored colors were the most easily obtainable. As a result, some years later we find it stated that, in the show ring in Great Britain, "the dominant colors are black-and-white, grey-and-white and shades of brindle-and-white, with a few solid blacks. Goldens are seen less often, which is a pity." The words are those of Mrs. L. G. Widdrington, President of the *Manchu Shih Tzu Society*, in one of the Society's newsletters.

It would seem certain that this scarcity of goldens accounts for the highly surprising omission of any special preference for that color in the British standard which appears to have been based on the situation prevailing at the time in England rather than on the Chinese ideal for the breed.

In the endeavor to secure a position of priority for the imperial color a leading part has been taken by Mrs. Audrey Fowler, who—without doubt bitterly regretting that her original two little 12-pound imports left no issue—has stressed that, according to the

Countess d'Anjou, honey, golden and gold-and-white were the most highly prized in China. Examples of this will be found in the British magazine, *Our Dogs*, December, 1961, page 41; the British *Shih Tzu News*, February, 1966, page 17; and the American *Shih Tzu News*, June, 1966, inside back cover.

Not only in color but also in appearance the Shih Tzu is supposed to resemble a lion, albeit a lion as pictured by Chinese who may never have set eyes on the real animal.

Stolidly Anglo-Saxon in appearance, too many Shih Tzu bear a much closer resemblance to the Cheshire cat as protrayed in children's editions of Louis Carroll's *Alice in Wonderland*. In such cases only the most strictly selective breeding can restore to succeeding generations the Oriental look. After passing through the "chrysanthemum" stage, for a time a Shih Tzu puppy can legitimately resemble a very cuddlesome Australian Koala Bear, but as adult it should be distinctively and unmistakably Chinese in appearance.

RELATIONSHIP TO THE PEKINGESE

Although some western scholars have questioned it, as we have seen it was quite certainly believed in China that the Shih Tzu were,

Because of his lifelong association with man the Shih Tzu is the peerless house dog. Here a group of dogs owned by Rev. and Mrs. D. Allan Easton relaxes at the family home. They are (l. to r.) Jigme, Ying, Yu-Lo, Tai-Tai, Trari (partially hidden), Li-Che, Ho-Ko, Dorje and Hwang. The Shih Tzu is as comfortable in our modern homes today as he was in the court of his Imperial masters of time gone by.

Chumulari Wu-Lo.

at least in part, Tibetan in origin. While such strongly established and widely held opinions may not be accurate sources of information regarding details, they are rarely without some foundation in fact.

For this reason I find myself personally unconvinced by Berthold Laufer's assertion that, after having "specially hunted for this purpose" through the available records, he could not "find, in fact, any instance in Chinese history of dogs having been exported from Tibet into China."

In any event, the Shih Tzu's Tibetan heritage is surely demonstrated by its appearance and by its close similarity—in certain respects—to the Lhasa Apso which undoubtedly hails from that country.

Also vigorously challenged by some western breeders today, but firmly believed by those in China who were in a better position to know, is the fact that the Shih Tzu from Tibet were on occasion interbred with the native Pekingese. For example, Volume III of Colonel Valentine Burkhardt's *Chinese Creeds and Customs* mentions this, distinguishing the Shih Tzu from the imperial lap dogs but pointing out that they were interbred. Parallel statements are to be found in V. W. F. Collier's *Dogs of China in Nature and Art*, on pages 164 and 186, as well as in *The Lhassa Lion Dog*, on pages 6–7, where Madame Lu takes the fact of cross-breeding for granted.

If this thought seems strange to western fanciers, it must be remembered that the Chinese did not breed by pedigree but rather

Young Diane Lindblom and her Chumulari P'eng Yu.

aimed to produce a type as close as possible to a picture before them.

Thus cross-breeding was apparently done sometimes to reduce the size of the Shih Tzu (Burkhardt), sometimes to improve the coat of the Pekingese (Collier), while Madame Lu suggests that it was also done to produce different types and colors.

This last might possibly explain the Princess Der Ling's reference to vain efforts by the Empress Dowager to reproduce a dog which "seemed a sort of outcast. His coloring was yellow and black, and his measurements were perfect. Her Majesty had spent much time to try and find a mate for him with the same markings, but during my time at court she did not succeed. It was one of her few failures."

It is also possible that the cross-breeding was designed to change the shape of the Tibetan dog's skull and to flatten the forehead, making it more lion-like in Chinese eyes. We refer to the article by Miss S. M. Lampson, entitled *Lion Dog of the Manchu Emperors*, in the British magazine, *Country Life*, June 14th, 1962, on page 1413. There Miss Lampson shares my view that "the Shih Tzu of China are unquestionably very close relations of the Apsos of Tibet."

Or again, since the eunuchs vied with one another in the production of exquisite little gems for the ladies of the imperial court, it may

Galloping, Toddie and Ting-a-Ling, three early Scandinavian Shih Tzu.

Fu Shu v.d. Oranje Manege, owned by Rev. and Mrs. D. Allan Easton and bred by Miss Eta Pauptit of the Netherlands. Fu Shu, a 9½ pound, gold and white male was considered an excellent show specimen on the Continent and easily made his Canadian Championship after his importation. A litter sister, Int. Ch. Freya Shu v.d. Oranje Manege, was best in show at the Zuidlaren International Show, 1969, under judge Mrs. Schoor over an entry of 1067 dogs.

well be that their "trade" secret was the occasional introduction of Pekingese blood. As has been suggested to me by a student of the subject, it is perfectly possible that little or nothing of this secret was known outside the servants' quarters.

Whether or not this last point be true, for one reason or another it seems undeniably true that Pekingese blood was on occasion introduced into the palace "Tibetans" or Shi Tzu Kou.

This is the justification for the "Peke cross," introduced in England in 1952, on one occasion, with the specific purpose of eliminating "certain faults in the breed," under the strictest possible controls, and with the full knowledge of the British Kennel Club and of the officials of the breed club at the time.

Chumulari Sheng-Li Che, a typically winsome Shih Tzu puppy seems to be reflecting on the breed's illustrious past while posing before an appropriate Chinese artifact.

Wei-Honey Gold of Elfann, owned by Rev. and Mrs. D. Allan Easton. Honey is a gold-colored bitch imported from England. She is the dam of the lovely American-bred Chumulari Trari, and is pictured here relaxing on a vacation trip to Alaska.

In fairness to all concerned, it must be remembered that there were very special reasons why it seemed necessary in England at that time to introduce the cross to produce "a new blood-line to be bred back to the original strain." The words are those of Mrs. Thelma Morgan, a founder member of the Manchu Shih Tzu Society and an enthusiastic supporter of the breed.

"If a World War, and a clamping down of trade afterwards had not prevented more stock being obtained," Mrs. Morgan recalled in 1966, "then I doubt whether a cross would have been either contemplated or allowed by the English Kennel Club." While this provides the immediate reason for the action taken at that time, very much more important is the fact that it can be amply explained

The Pekingese Cross of 1952 was introduced as follows:

Tee-ni Tim of Michelcombe
(dog)

	Sire : Fu Chuan of Elfann (Shih Tzu)	
Shih Wei Tzu of Elfann (bitch)		Sire : Ch. Choo-ling (Shih Tzu)
	Dam : Yu Honey of Elfann	
		Sire : Philadelphus Suti T'Sun of Elfann (Pekingese)
Mu-Ho (bitch)		Dam : Yu Sunny of Elfann
		Dam : Elfann Fenling of Yram (Shih Tzu)
Third Cross	Second Cross	First Cross

Except for Ch. Choo-ling, who belonged to Lady Brownrigg, all the dogs concerned belong to Miss Evans.

After the third cross, all subsequent generations were given a Class I Certificate by the Kennel Club (England) and accepted as purebred Shih Tzu. The American Kennel Club required three or more generations. A great-grandson of Tee-ni Tim of Michelcombe, Fu-ling of Clystevale—imported into Sweden in 1958—was six generations from the original cross (1/54th Pekingese)—one generation short of the very stringent requirement of the American Kennel Club.

and defended in the light of the background and history of the Shih Tzu.

The cross was made under the meticulously careful supervision of Miss E. M. Evans, a distinguished and highly successful breeder of Pekingese, whose growing love for the Shih Tzu led her to the conviction that this courageous step was necessary for the betterment of the breed in England. In defense of her action, she explained that the Shih Tzu in her homeland were too large, too high on leg, too long of muzzle with very bad pigmentation and too closely inbred.

Shebo Schunde of Hungjao, a black dog owned by Mrs. Sheila Bode and bred by Major-General A. Telfer-Smollett. Sire: Wu; dam: Ishuh Tzu. Schunde's dam was a gold-brindle and white imported by the Major-General directly from China in 1948. Mated to Mao Mao of Lhakang, a liver and white, Schunde threw a clear gold and white bitch with black points. This line was later to produce the first solid apricot and gold Shih Tzu to be whelped in England.

This view of the Imperial Summer Palace on the lake a few miles outside of Peking will give the reader some idea of the glory of the Manchu court. All available references tell us that the Shih Tzu was an integral part of this sumptuous life, and it is not very difficult to imagine that this was indeed the case.

For this reason Miss Evans of set purpose bred a Shih Tzu bitch, Elfann Fenling of Yram, with a beautifully coated black-and-white Pekingese, Philadelphus Suti T'Sun of Elfann "with perfect pigment, large dark eyes, whose only fault was *straight* legs."

The offspring of this one and only cross were bred back to purebred Shih Tzu, only one from each generation being selected for this purpose, and the successive breedings were fully recorded with the British Kennel Club in the crossbred register. With the fourth generation, containing only one-sixteenth Pekingese ancestry, the dogs were recognized by the British Kennel Club as purebred Shih Tzu and were registered and shown as such.

Published fourteen years after, the *Manchu Shih Tzu Society News Letter*, March, 1966, on pages 5–6–7, contains a clear summation by Miss Evans who writes that, by that time, British breeders "with the cross are greatly in the majority and their owners appear to be quite happy with their dogs, and there are now 15 champions with the cross. Certain improved characteristics have been claimed—especially pigmentation and the correct shorter leg."

There can be little doubt that the majority of informed Shih Tzu breeders, both in Great Britain and elsewhere, would now agree that this very carefully controlled cross was good for the breed and had ample historical justification.

According to the *Manchu Shih Tzu Society News Letter* of May/June 1968, something of the "Peke Cross" was introduced into the Scandinavian line ten years before this with the importation into Sweden of the English-bred "Fu-Ling of Clystvale." This stud was exchanged for the Swedish-bred "Jungfaltets Jung Ming," an exchange of bloodlines which is said to have done much to improve both Scandinavian and English stock.

Mrs. Erma Jungefeldt has written an interesting account of their visit to England in 1958 when she and her husband attended championship shows at Blackpool and Windsor, looking for "a small Shih Tzu as a stud dog for our own kennel and the Shih Tzu breed in Sweden."

Another view of one of the precincts of the Summer Palace. In the right foreground is the "Sacred Cow." It was believed that if one touched this a cure would be effected for many illnesses.

"The Shih Tzu were mostly terribly big, near 18 pounds in weight." Mrs. Jungefeldt recalls, "Suddenly we found a small black-and-white youth by the name of Fu-Ling of Clystvale, owned by Mrs. Longden. We saw Fu-Ling at both shows. He was a little bit bashful and not a real shower, but of real good size, low on legs, a wonderfully strong chest and with a weight of about nine and a half pounds, the smallest one we had seen in England."

Fu-Ling proved an outstanding success in the Scandinavian show ring, not only by his own successes but also by those of his offspring. Quickly winning his Swedish championship with very favorable comments from the judges, he eventually sired "more than 23 champions and challenge certificate winners, many best in show and group winners, and his sons and daughters have won in several countries of Europe and also in the United States."

Jungfaltets Jung-Ming, owned by Mrs. Longden and bred by Mrs. Carl-Olof Jungefeldt of Sweden with whom he is shown here. Jung-Ming was one of the two studs involved in the exchange between England and Sweden. Mrs. Jungefeldt received Mrs. Longden's Fu-Ling of Clystvale to bring certain improvements to the breed on the Continent.

Swedish Ch. Fu-Ling of Clystvale, owned by Mrs. Carl-Olof Jungefeldt and bred by Mrs. Longden. Fu-Ling was imported from England to Sweden in 1958. This 9½ pound black and white dog was widely used as a stud in Scandinavia and has produced many Champions for European Fanciers.

At the age of eleven, this famous sire was described as "still going strong and admired for his low weight and small type." Clearly Fu-Ling of Clystvale's distant relationship to Miss Evan's Pekingese had done him no harm, to say the least!

So far as the United States is concerned, as has been made clear in a statement issued by the *Manchu Shih Tzu Society*, Shih Tzu imported from England should be at least seven generations removed from the original cross, which means—in other words—that the three-generation export pedigree should not carry the name of any dog registered with the British Kennel Club as a cross breed.

The courtyard of the Imperial Palace, Peking. For many centuries only the privileged few were allowed access here. It was in this stronghold of mystery and seclusion that the Eunuchs conducted the breeding programs which brought about the regal Shi Tzu.

Similarly the three-generation export pedigree should not list the name of any import, so that Shih Tzu coming from Europe to the United States should be at least four generations removed from those brought out of China.

This clarification by the Manchu Shih Tzu Society is borne out by a letter from Mr. John Brownell, Assistant to the Executive Vice-President of the American Kennel Club, addressed to Miss Olga Dakan and dated June 14th, 1963. As the years go by, however, these questions should become matters of purely academic interest.

Defending the Pekingese cross made by Miss Evans in 1952 to improve the quality of the Shih Tzu in England, other fanciers on both sides of the Atlantic have been quick to point out that there are "many breeds which to improve type have had another breed introduced into them." One asserts that the Cavalier King Charles had two breeds crossed into the strain in its early days. Another maintains that the Affenpinscher and Standard Schnauzer together produced the Miniature Schnauzer, the Australian and Yorkshire

This lovely protrait by Jeffrey Dali (nephew of Salvator Dali) is of Chumulari Trari. The artist has beautifully translated the charm of the Shih Tzu on canvas so that all can appreciate the elegant beauty of a breed that was described in old China as "exquisite little gems."

Terriers the Silky Terrier, while "in England the Bearded Collie was crossed into the Old English Sheepdog to reduce the size of the latter," and Cocker Spaniel blood apparently introduced to save the Sussex Spaniel from the threat of extinction.

On such matters every Shih Tzu fancier is entitled to express his own point of view. Those who claim to have "pure" stock "without Pekingese blood," however, as is occasionally advertised, somehow give the impression that they believe the Shih Tzu to have dropped straight from heaven in its present form! Certainly no one who has ever lived in China would make the mistake of assuming that court breeding practices were similar to those rigidly enforced by a modern European or North American Kennel Club.

THE SHIH TZU'S TIBETAN HERITAGE

If the views just expressed seem controversial, it cannot be too strongly emphasized that they represent a relatively mild echo of

There is little argument that the Shih Tzu and the Lhasa Apso are closely related breeds. These five-month-old Chumulari puppies, with their unbanded topknots, seem very like their Tibetan cousins.

Chumulari Yae Jin, owned by Mrs. Eve Jorgensen. This popular West Coast stud is of a stunning dark brindle color with gold highlights.

opinions expressed by at least one authority in China during the period when the Shih Tzu was first becoming known to the western world. Mr. A. de C. Sowerby, editor of the *China Journal* of Shanghai and an obviously knowledgeable dog-lover, wrote in the February, 1933 issue beginning on page 112—

"It is in our opinion that the Tibetan Lion Dog is the result of a cross between the Lhassa Terrier and the Pekingese, which has arisen out of the mixing of the two breeds both in Tibet and China, since the dogs of each country have been taken to the other from time to time by tribute envoys and officials. The cross in Tibet, that has been taken out of that country by way of India, has been called the Apso, while the cross in Peking has been called the Tibetan Poodle or Lion Dog. Doubtless the Tibetan cross has more of the Lhassa Terrier in it, while the Chinese cross has more of the Pekingese."

The Lotus Court at the Summer Palace outside Peking.

Finally, in June 1937, after reading a book called *Pure Bred Dogs*, published in the United States. Mr. Sowerby commented in his periodical on page 365—

"A picture of a Lhassa Terrier is given that helps clear up for us in China the difficulty surrounding the identities of so-called 'Tibetans.' This apparently is the 'Apso' of English fanciers, and it may at once be distinguished from the Tibetan Lion Dog which we get in Peiping by its much longer and straighter legs."

"Old China Hands" will have no difficulty in understanding Mr. Sowerby's approach to the problem and will agree that he is probably right in his conclusions.

As has already been noted, when first imported into England in 1930 the Shih Tzu were classified as Apsos, the two breeds not being distinguished until 1934. Noting the existence of "considerable confusion," and obviously concerned that any "said to be" Chinese Lion Dog should challenge the longer established Pekingese, a commentator was quick to point out that the newcomers were very definitely not lion-like in looks. This criticism might still be levelled at some English Shih Tzu today and their appearance has done much to create confusion with the Lhasa Apso.

In this respect the Shih Tzu of Scandinavian background are in a different category. I have never heard of any dogs of this line being mistaken for Lhasa Apso, even after importation into the United States, their distinctive appearance—like that of many other English Shih Tzu—being such that there is no likelihood of confusion.

So far as the United States is concerned, seven early imports from England are said to have been registered as Apsos between 1942 and 1952. Steps were taken to prevent further mistakes of this nature, once the error was known, the British Shih Tzu Club expressing their fear of "disastrous" cross-breeding in the United States and agreeing to encourage future American purchasers to do everything possible "to avoid any further confusion between the Shih Tzu and Lhasa Apso in the U.S.A."

Although the two breeds have been kept completely separate for many years, as recently as April 7th, 1966, it was reported in the *New York Times* that "one obstacle (in the way of recognition) was

The coat of the Shih Tzu when properly cared for is a thing of beauty and an object of admiration to all that see it. A pin brush such as is shown here is the best grooming tool for the Shih Tzu.

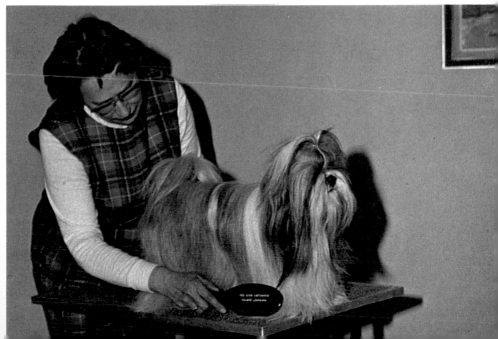

that the Shih Tzu strongly resembles the Lhasa Apso, also a Tibetan breed that already was in the American Kennel Club's official family of purebreds. The American Kennel Club needs assurance that the two are separate breeds."

The situation was not helped by the photograph accompanying the article, presumably supplied by a well-meaning fancier, showing a dog which bore a striking resemblance to a Lhasa Apso. By a strange coincidence, apart from a difference in position and color and a slightly different combing of the head furnishings, it was virtually identical to a Lhasa Apso which had been pictured in the same newspaper almost exactly one year previously, on April 8th, 1965. So long as fanciers continue to give prominence to Shih Tzu of this type, apparently believing that the breed need only be shaggy and without any distinctive Chinese characteristics, confusion with the Apso seems inevitable.

In this regard there is much wisdom in the advice of Mrs. Irene Booth, editor of the *Manchu Shih Tzu Society News Letter*, who wrote in the December, 1965, issue: "We help by always showing the Shih Tzu with the long sweep of hair on the top of the head tied with a rubber band into a top knot. The hair above the head then fanning out into a 'palm tree.' The Apso, on the other hand, has its long hair of the head parted in the centre, then mingling with the ear featherings."

An illuminating discussion of the relationship between the two breeds is to be found in the Shih Tzu column, *Popular Dogs* of October and November, 1968, where my guest columnist was an English fancier, who has made an extensive sudy of Tibetan-Chinese breeds. An Apso breeder of international repute, this lady is on the committee of the British Tibetan Apso Club for which she is a listed judge. So important are her observations that I repeat them at length—

"Shih Tzu people even now meet the question, 'Is it a Tibetan?' Apso breeders are asked, It's a Shih Tzu, isn't it? That confusion still exists about the two breeds poses some questions. Are we careful enough to emphasize the distinctions of the two breeds types? Do we really appreciate the subtleties of the different characteristics of Chinese Shih Tzu and Tibetan Apso?

"In those indications of their countries of origin lies the key to it. That both Shih Tzu and Apso have common ancestry is highly

One of the distinguishing points of the Shih Tzu is the way in which his topknot is handled. Instead of falling down over his eyes as is the custom with the Lhasa Apso, the hair is caught up in an elastic and fanned out so that it has the distinct resemblance to a palm tree.

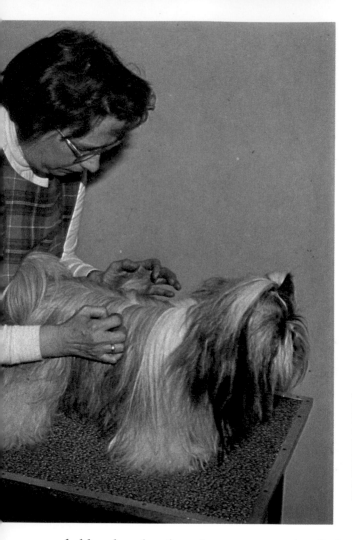

The Shih Tzu coat
is parted down the
back from the top
of the neck to the
root of the tail.
For the show ring
it is very important
for this part to be
absolutely straight
for its entire length.

probable; that they have become two quite distinct breeds is certainly the result of selectivity by man, and, even more important, the different climates and environments of the lands in which they developed.

"There is good reason to suppose that the cult of the 'Lion Dog' began in Tibet around Lhasa, and preceded the similar cult in China by several centuries.

"The earliest 'Lion Dogs' in Tibet were probably long-haired and small and somewhat similar to the Maltese in type. As the cultural

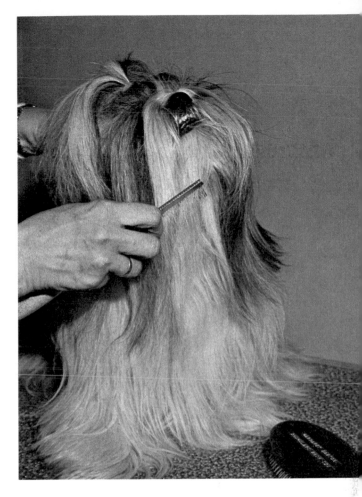

"Agony" might be the title of this photo judging from the model's expression. Actually a Shih Tzu needs careful, frequent grooming to always look his very best. Regularly carried out grooming need not take too long or be hard on the dog. A coat that has been neglected however amounts to hard work for the owner and much unnecessary discomfort for the dog.

and religious ties between Tibet and China ebbed and flowed, over the centuries, no doubt the exchange of dogs became a two-way affair. The Chinese most certainly interbred their small dogs, of which there were many varieties, with the long-haired Tibetans, and something similar no doubt occurred in Tibet.

"The outcome of this interbreeding were the Shih Tzu—which the Chinese are said to call the 'Tibetan Lion Dog'—and the Apso which the Tibetans refer to as the *Apso Seng Kyi* or 'Apso Lion Dog'.

"The Chinese would undoubtedly try to retain the characteristics they admired—the unnaturally short face and broad head, the wide barrel-like chest, the low-to-the-ground look.

"The Tibetans, on the other hand, would not be able to hold these characteristics, because of the climate and environment of the land itself. Tibet is an area of high altitudes, and Lhasa, the real home of the Apso, is high. The very short face with its restricted nasal development, and the heavy body and short legs, would be at a disadvantage in these conditions, and could not survive as fixed characteristics of a breed. They would adapt, naturally, to the environment, so that Tibetans would produce a dog slightly modified from the Chinese dog of a similar ancestry.

"If one views the Chinese and Tibetan dogs on a scale of progression from the natural dog to the most unnatural, the importance of these distinctions can be appreciated more readily.

"The Tibetan Terrier is probably the nearest to the basic canine, a long-headed type, compact but natural in conformation.

Ko Ko of Shu Lin (left) Pia Mia of Shu Lin (center) and Ta Kao Josephine of Ssu-Chi, all owned by Colonel and Mrs. David Langdon. Ko Ko and Pia were bred by Dr. and Mrs. Sidney Bashore and Josephine is a homebred sired by Ko Ko out of Pia.

The Lhasa Apso is longer on leg and has a longer muzzle than the Shih Tzu. He was bred larger and was more generally suited to Tibetan living conditions than court dogs of China.

The Shih Tzu combines certain characteristics of the Lhasa Apso and the Pekingese in his appearance. He stands midway between the two breeds in many particulars. Muzzle and leg length being two features in particular.

The Pekingese is the most extreme of the oriental dogs. He has the shortest muzzle, most bowed legs and the longest body.

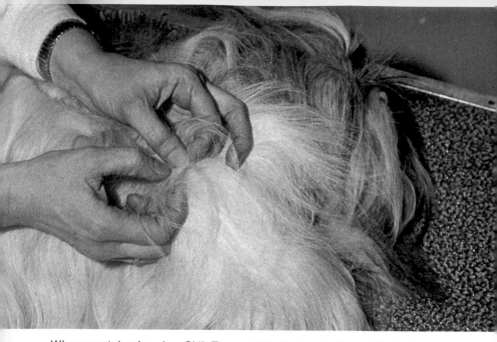

When a mat develops in a Shih Tzu coat it is best worked out with the fingers a little at a time. Attempting to force the mat out or cutting it out will mar the coat and it may take many months for the coat to be fully restored.

"Then comes the Apso, which shows the influence of some 'foreign type.' This influence results in a small dog, shorter in the leg than its terrier relative, shorter in the nose—approximately $1\frac{1}{2}$ inches, with proportions of one third to two thirds of the whole head, as against the terrier two inch nose and half and half proportions. The teeth and jaw formation reveal the shortening of the face, the lower incisors being set in a straight line, and not in a curve as in the basic dog. The eyes are not oblique, though not globular, and are more frontally placed. The skull is a concession to the Tibetan environment and is narrow, though not as narrow as that of the terrier.

"Compare this with the Shih Tzu, in which the 'foreign' characteristics are more emphasized than in the Apso, and reveal its Chinese origin. The chest is wider, the leg is shorter still, and although it must appear straight, the foreleg can have a slight bow to the upper part (provided feet do not turn out and the elbows are in). The nose is further reduced, to approximately an inch, or about one-fourth to three-fourths of the whole head. The skull is broad and the whole appearance of the head is short and broad. The movement is strong and free, but more arrogant and not so floating and agile as the Apso.

"The Chinese characteristics in the Shih Tzu, however, are not nearly so exaggerated as in the Pekingese, in which they become the furthest removed of all from the basic, natural dog."

Smallness in size must have been fashionable and something of a status symbol in both Apso and Shih Tzu, the column continues, provided the essential characteristics and type were maintained. In this regard, the Chinese breeding program was more effective than the Tibetan, being less casual, although in both breeds, in the writer's opinion, "you get true miniatures."

Correct use of the fine comb around the face furnishings will impart the typical mandarin look to a Shih Tzu. This expression is an essential breed characteristic and the owner should know how to bring this out in his dog.

After the publication of this article, I was challenged about a suggestion in it, mdae by the writer, that the *original* Tibetan Lion Dog, bred by monks in the monasteries many centuries ago, was probably extinct, the present Apso being a modification of it with some Chinese blood.

According to his comments in the February, 1933, issue of the *China Journal* of Shanghai, quoted earlier, Mr. Sowerby would have endorsed this suggestion whole-heartedly, and the views of such an authority on Oriental breeds are not to be taken lightly.

Although I have not seen it personally, I am most reliably informed that strong support for the above suggestion will be found in a letter by Mr. Brian Vesey-Fitzgerald which appeared under the Tibetan Breed notes in the British magazine, *Our Dogs*, of July 17th, 1953. According to an informant in whom I have the utmost confidence, this letter ran—

"Such information as I have came from Kusho Chang Fa (Ringang) one of the old ruling caste of Tibet, and a former minister, who was educated at Rugby a (well known English boarding school), and was a great friend of mine.

"As I understand it, Apso means dog, no more than that. Once it used to mean Temple dog, and in that connection came to mean Lion Dog (a temple synonym) but that was a long time ago. I have always understood that it was about 1650 that three temple dogs, holy dogs, were sent to China and that from these three came the Shih Tzu. About 100 years later, so I have always understood, the then Dalai Lama (and up to that time the temple dog had been his special property), gave some away to distinguished visitors, who were Russians. These dogs were stolen before they had reached the border, and about the same time, during a civil upheaval, a good many more disappeared from the Dalai Lama's monastery and reappeared in various parts of the country. That was the end of the Temple or Lion Dog, the Apso. From that time onwards all sorts of small dogs bearing some resemblance, however vague, to the Apso of old became known as Apso. It was the end of the temple dog but it was the start of the monastery dog and also the caravan dog."

The contents of this letter may not be wholly accurate, not only because the English writer could have been confused regarding detail but even more because most of the information must have been passed down from one generation to another for some two

Chumulari Liu Mang, owned by Mr. Joseph Hochrein. This male is gold and white with black tippings. He is eighteen months old in this photo and shows a beautiful coat for such a young dog.

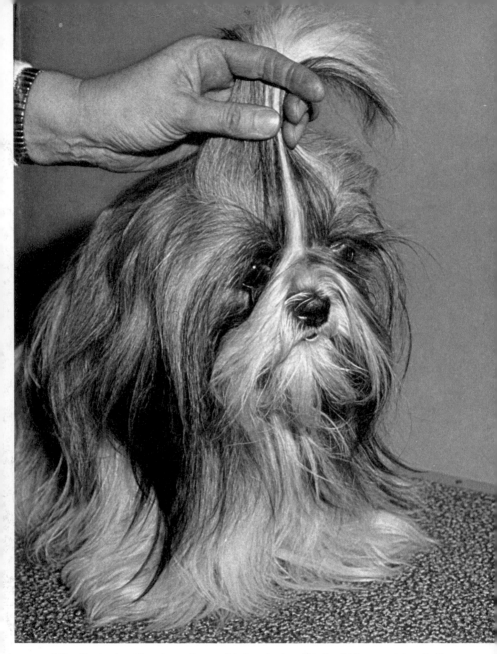

After the topknot has been thoroughly brushed out it should be caught up in the hand and tied back with an elastic. When properly done the result will be the desired "palm tree" effect.

centuries. For example, it is questionable whether "Apso" does mean only "dog," there being some reason to believe that it means also "goat-like" or "shaggy."

However none of the parties concerned could have had the slightest reason to fabricate the story regarding the extinction of the original Holy Dog, least of all the Tibetans who would have been much more likely to conceal the fact that there had been any break in the direct line of succession. In my opinion the highly unexpected nature of the story is itself convincing evidence of its truth.

If this is correct, neither the present day Apso nor the Shih Tzu can be regarded as "pure" representatives of the historic Tibetan Holy Dog, both being the products of interbreeding in various degrees. In any event the two are clearly historically related, the Apso having developed along distinctively Tibetan lines, while the Shih Tzu, through climate, environment, and human planning, has become essentially Chinese.

Good head furnishings, a long, dense coat covering the entire body, a well-plumed gaily carried tail and a proud bearing are some of the more important essentials typical of the Shih Tzu and responsible for making him so highly regarded among dog fanciers.

As I wrote in *Popular Dogs* in December, 1965— "Closely related in the distant past, for centuries the two breeds have developed along totally different lines. While the Apso remained in the remote fastness of Tibet, from which it came to us recently by way of India, long years ago the Shih Tzu was taken eastward to share in the life of the Chinese court.

"In Scandinavia, where it was brought directly from Peking 33 years ago, the Shih Tzu is classified and shown as a Toy. Undoubtedly this is a correct interpretation of the Chinese ideal. How else can we explain the careful introduction of the Pekingese strain, except that it was designed to make the larger mountain watchdog more suitable for the imperial drawing room? This is part of the breed's unique heritage of which we have no cause to be ashamed.

Norwegian Ch. Zizi's Tara, owned and bred by Mrs. Ruth Laakso. Tara is pictured here at age eight months frolicking in deep snow, a pastime most Shih Tzu seem to enjoy.

Ch. Maya Wong of Lhakang, owned by Mrs. L. G. Widdrington. Although she is of the larger size, Maya Wong produced four of the smaller type puppies in a litter of six sired by Wen Shu of Lhakang.

For all his lion-hearted courage, the ideal Shih Tzu is essentially a small dog.

Both physically and in temperament, there is an unmistakeable difference between the cautious guard dog from the hidden Himalayas and his gaily topknotted little relative who comes as a household pet from the much more sophisticated palaces of Peking."

It should be noted that the traffic appears to have operated in both directions, Pekingese and other palace dogs being on occasion taken, or sent as gifts, to Tibet where they were interbred with the native variety. Although it is improbable that the process was as carefully controlled as at the imperial court, there is some evidence that it did lead to the appearance of dogs with strong similarities in character to the Peking Shih Tzu.

In the year 1900 at the hill station of Murree in India there was shown for the first time as a separate breed a variety known as Lhassa or Bhutan Terriers, sometimes called Lhassa Spaniels, their place of origin presumably indicated by their name. Of these dogs it is written that "they are most lovable little fellows, clever as performing dogs, devoted companions, exceedingly quaint, and with a charm of their own."

They are described as natural beggars, so much so that the Princess of Wales, later to become Queen Alexandra, remarked on seeing one on exhibit in England, "That little dog is begging to leave the show."

Samten v. Tschomo-Lungma, owned by Mrs. Erika Geusendam, is a winner of four International Certificates in Germany and in Belgium. Samten is a typical representative of Mrs. Geusendam's line, a line that is entirely based on Scandinavian foundation stock and is completely unrelated to any of the English bloodlines.

Capella Taitzung, bred and owned by Mr. Antti Seppälä of Finland.

In fact, it is said, nothing could have been further from the truth, the little performer being in his element!

Regarding this breed Mrs. McLaren Morrison, an early importer and authority, wrote in 1904, "I would like to see much more attention paid to size, to which the natives of the country they come from attach the greatest importance. There really should be two classes for them, over and under a certain weight."

As the limits were then set at 8–15 pounds, presumably Mrs. McLaren Morrison would have liked a division at 11 or 12 pounds. Even more important is the fact she clearly saw that two different types were developing, a large and a small. The latter were the most highly prized and the hardest to obtain in Tibet.

No such division into two weight classes was made at that time, in spite of Mrs. McLaren Morrison's urging, but the question of size was to arise 62 years later with the comments that the breed in England, by then known as Tibetan Spaniels, was "not dainty enough," being "heavier" and "bigger all over." At about the same time another English writer suggested that there was "a strong resemblance" between the Tibetan Spaniel and "some Apso." Reference to this will be found in the English *Dog World* of February 11th and May 27th, 1966.

In a discussion of the background of the Tibetan Spaniel, to be found in *About Our Dogs* by A. Croxton Smith, we are told that Mrs. McLaren Morrison regarded it as "ancestor of the Pekingese. Others say it owes its origin to the Chinese dogs, which were taken into Tibet and crossed with the Lhassa Terriers. He is a small toy, standing on short legs and having a rather long body. The legs are

Ch. Soong of Lhakang, owned and bred by Mrs. L. G. Widdrington, is a ten-pound black and white bitch. She incorporates the Swedish line through Jungfaltets Jung-Ming and is an outstanding representative of the smaller type.

Ch. Ta-Chi of Taishan, a fourteen-pound dog owned by the late Lady Brownrigg. He was the first Shih Tzu Champion in Britain, and in the opinion of Mrs. Widdrington, "he has never been bettered."

straighter than those of the Pekingese and the jaws are of a natural state."

Describing the breed in the 1930s, after "over thirty years experience of judging Tibetan Spaniels," the Honorary Secretary of the Kennel Club of India wrote in *Hutchinson's Dog Encyclopaedia*—

"The Standard might be put into a few words, viz. 'A Pekingese gone wrong,'—the face is not flat, and the muzzle is as prominent as in any ordinary breed; the skull, instead of being flat, is more rounded. The body is long for the dog's height, the coat like a Pekingese, the plume not so full as the Peke but the tail lighter feathered and curled over the back; legs short, but the forelegs quite straight;

Wei-Honey Gold of Elfann, bred by Miss E. M. Evans of England, imported and owned by Rev. and Mrs. D. Allan Easton.

chest not wide like the Peke, the body much the same from the chest to the loin, which of course is quite different from the Peke."

"Surely that is a Pekingese gone wrong!" is accepted by another writer in the Encyclopaedia as "the very natural mistake most people make when they see (a Tibetan Spaniel) for the first time." Clearly there must be some relationship to the palace dogs although the full facts are hard to find.

In the English *Dog World* of December 24th, 1965, some illuminating comments on the subject will be found, based on a conversation with Mrs. Annie Foy, an 89-year-old lady who spent her youth in Sikkim and Bhutan on the borders of India and Tibet. Describing the Tibetan Spaniels which Mrs. Foy saw in Bhutan the article runs, "There were long-nosed and long-coated types and also some short-muzzled ones, but these were, even so, longer in muzzle than a Pekingese—but the different types were in different monasteries, and the shorter muzzles came from nearest to the Chinese borders."

As was pointed out in an authoritative article in the British *Kennel Gazette* of August, 1934, the influence of the Chinese dogs brought to Tibet was affected by the fact that there were no standardized types in that country. "This results in no very specialised, or as one might perhaps say, unnatural dogs being bred there."

In other words, in the more crude conditions prevailing in Tibet, the Shih Tzu type of dogs tended to lose their refined man-made characteristics and to become larger, coarser, and more terrier-like in appearance. Keeping the Palace Lion Dogs small in size and short in features, two characteristics which distinguish them from the Apso, requires the most strictly selective and careful breeding. This is as true in England or America today as it was in old-time China and Tibet.

As a surprising footnote, it was reported in 1934 that the late Dalai Lama had possessed "a Pekingese (of a sort)." Strangely enough, however, his favorite house pet was a Dachshund!

That there were also Shih Tzu-like dogs in Tibet during this period is confirmed by the evidence of the Venerable Akong Rimpoche, Abbot of Lhakang, now at the Tibetan Monastic Centre in Dumfriesshire, Scotland. On seeing an English-bred Shih Tzu of 18–20 pounds, the Abbot commented that he had seen similar dogs in the hands of Tibetan noble families but much smaller and with coats sweeping the ground.

CHAPTER III

THE QUESTION OF SIZE —
SOME HISTORICAL FACTS

As has already been noted, according to Colonel Burkhardt the imperial Shih Tzu were occasionally inter-bred with the Pekingese "to reduce the size." The Colonel wrote from first hand experience of Peking Palace life not long after the 1912 revolution and before rising nationalistic feelings made the presence of foreign military officers unwelcome.

Published some time later, the preface to Madame Lu's booklet expresses a similar opinion, apparently written by someone connected with the newly formed Peking Kennel Club. The *Peiping Chronicle* of May 17th, 1936, describes the translator of the booklet as Mr. C. S. K. Chou but unfortunately does not identify the writer of the preface. Referring to the "Lhassa Lion Dogs," the passage runs—"There is also every evidence to show that these dogs have been bred down from a larger-sized breed and this theory is supported by the great variety of size and weight which is found in this class of dogs."

Although we are told that the Empress Dowager discouraged the use of "cruel practices" to stunt the growth of the dogs, the two quotations above would seem to imply that the imperial eunuchs tried to keep the Shih Tzu small by strictly selective breeding. Such selective breeding met with the approval of the Empress, according to Mrs. Dixey, but it is clear that it was not always successful so far as the production of uniform size was concerned.

This appears to have been especially true in the years immediately following the 1912 revolution during which Colonel Burkhardt tells us that "the mating was rather haphazard." Not surprisingly, some 20 years later we find the complaint in Madame Lu's booklet regard-

For most of the time the Shih Tzu has been known to the west there have been two distinct sizes within the breed. This has often made for a great deal of controversy among the proponents of each. That a certain amount of confusion still exists is evident from the fact that in Britain the breed is classed in the Utility group, in Canada the Non-Sporting group and in the U.S.A. the Toy group.

ing "the great variety of size and weight." The same could have been said of the imperial goldfish which must also have started to increase in size with the break-down of controlled breeding.

Strong support for this viewpoint is to be found in the *China Weekly Chronicle* of June 10th, 1934. Reporting Peiping's First International Dog Show, held on June 7th of the same year, the paper states that the Lhassa Lion Dogs were, "on the whole, disappointing in spite of their numbers, showing too much deviation from the standard, especially in size, suggesting the necessity of careful breeding to the standard in future." Since the Peking Kennel Club's official standard did not come until four years later it is uncertain what standard is referred to at this earlier date. Presumably it was a tentative one, based on what was known of the Lion Dog's background at that time.

I have since received from a Norwegian fancier a copy of a highly

Si-Kiang's Jody's Tidbie Toodle, owned by Miss Jody Lieberman and bred by the late Ingrid Colwell. This fine gold and white male is shown here with his mistress.

Rev. and Mrs. D. Allan Easton at home with Ch. Chumulari Ying Ying (left), Jemima of Lhakang (center) and Swiss, Czechoslovakian and Canadian Ch. Tangra v. Tschomo-Lungma.

important article which I have been trying to trace for more than two years. Although the name is not given, almost certainly it was written by Dr. Walter Young, author of *Some Canine Breeds of Asia.*

Published in Peiping shortly before the first Peking Kennel Club Show, the article begins, "at least as common as good Pekingese in Peiping are the Tibetans, the shock-headed long-coated little dogs which came to China during the Manchu dynasty as gifts from the grand lamas at Lhasa."

It is a "novel little breed," the writer continues, complaining that at that time, "no effort is made to distinguish what is quite evidently two distinct types, one considerably larger and higher on the leg than the other."

Mrs. Margaret Easton with Wei-Honey Gold of Elfann (left) and Si-Kiang's Tashi. This photograph was taken during a 10,000 mile camping trip to Alaska. The Easton entourage during this trip included Rev. and Mrs. Easton, their two young sons and two dogs in addition to the ones pictured. While in Western Canada the Eastons were asked if they were travelling with a performing animal act!

"They are commonly bred by Chinese fanciers who, to be sure, have not publicised the fact. And although there are no commercial kennels of a respectable character which breed these dogs, specimens of mixed merit, both of the large and the small varieties, may occasionally be seen at the disappointing dog markets at Lung Fu Ssu and Hu Kuo Ssu on fair days, either 'bred by exhibitor', or otherwise acquired."

At that date the writer was prepared to accept the placing of the breed in the non-sporting group, but it must be remembered that this was almost eighteen months before the return of the Princess Der Ling to Peking. Until she came on the scene and shared her knowledge with the Countess d'Anjou, fanciers in the city had no means of finding out the full truth about the palace dogs of old. Indeed the writer of this article admits that at that time there was much confusion about the breed.

"Probably not one in ten owning specimens of such dogs in

Int. Ch. Bjorneholms Lulu and her son Int. Ch. Bjorneholms Wu-Ling. Both of these fine Shih Tzu were bred and owned by Miss Astrid Jeppesen of Denmark.

Peiping," he acknowledges frankly, "is able to give its correct breed name, or even to distinguish it from the popular Pekingese."

The writer himself goes so far as to assert that the Empress Dowager "seems to have been unsuccessful in breeding these Tibetans." This statement, which we now know to be wholly incorrect, betrays a complete lack of accurate information at that time regarding the imperial dogs.

What is important is that the article fully confirms our theory regarding the existence of two types of Shih Tzu in Peking, at least so far as the 1930's are concerned, one "of the very small variety, in size more or less similar to the Pekingese," the other larger and apparently closely resembling what we now call the Apso, although "smaller with shorter legs."

It should be noted that the writer is also aware of "many cases of crossing" of Shih Tzu and Pekingese.

Said to be "sometimes indiscriminately called Lhassa Terriers or Apsos," the Lhassa Lion Dogs formed "the largest breed class in the show." Few details are given other than that "the dog class was won by a pure-bred Lhassa whose two half sisters also won the puppy class." The breed does not appear to have been put into any Group, but there is some indication that it was in a measure asso-

Scandinavian Ch. Zizi's Lhamo, a gold and white bitch owned by Mrs. Ruth Laakso.

A first for Shih Tzu, a first in the history of American Dog Shows; Ch. Chumulari Ying-Ying is shown taking Best in Show at the New Brunswick Kennel Club, September 1969. This was the first time the breed was shown in regular classes in America and the first time a win of this magnitude was scored by a newly recognized breed on the first day of recognition. Ying took this banner win under judge James Trullinger, handler John J. Marsh.

ciated with "the Novelty Class including Asiatic breeds for which the western official standards are either wanting or inadequate." Regarding this the evidence is confused.

Since very few names are given in the report, it is impossible to say whether or not the Countess d'Anjou's Shih Tzu appeared at this first Peking Show but it seems unlikely. Certainly if she had been recognized at that date as an authority on the breed, it is probable that some mention would have been made of the fact. We do know that her friendship with the Princess Der Ling must have originated considerably later, as the Princess only returned to Peking on October 3rd, 1935, "after an absence of nearly ten years." Prior to that date it seems clear that the Countess had no special source of information about the breed.

At the next Peiping International Dog Show, held on June 8th, 1935, several Shih Tzu dogs, bitches, and puppies were exhibited.

A British lion and three Chinese lions of Lhakang breeding in an interesting study taken at Newton Hall, the home of Mrs. L. G. Widdrington. The very oriental appearance of the Shi Tzu is well demonstrated here.

On this occasion the *China Weekly Chronicle* reported enthusiastically next day that "one of the most sensational entries was a Lhassa Terrier, an excellent, small, black-and-white bitch, owned by Mrs. Kun Chin, which took an amazing number of blue ribbons and cups."

Named "Shiao Ya," which could mean "Little Duck" or "Little Bud," this bitch won the cup for Best bitch in Show presented by the British Minister to China, His Excellency Sir Alexander Cadogan. Shiao Ya also won ribbons for being Best Lhassa Lion Dog bitch and Best of Breed, and cups for being the best Chinese-owned entry in the Show and the Best Non-Sporting bitch—there is no mention of any class for "Toys" or "Small Dogs."

A large and enthusiastic crowd attended the day-long show at which a panel of eleven judges officiated, all apparently European or American and including the Count d'Anjou.

The Lhassas of Madame Wilden, wife of the French Minister to China, are also described as being "exceptionally beautiful dogs, from the layman's standpoint." A dog of Madame Wilden's was second to one owned by Madame Lu, almost certainly the author of the "Lhassa Lion Dog," while a bitch owned by the Count d'Anjou came second to Mrs. Kun Chin's outstanding specimen.

There may be significance in the fact that the bitch which is unidentified, was registered in the Count d'Anjou's name and that it is he who appears most active in Peking Kennel Club affairs at this time. Although the Countess must also have been interested, is it too much to suggest that her full involvement dates from the time that she learned the full details of the Shih Tzu's fascinating history from the Princess who came to Peking almost exactly four months after the 1935 show? We shall never know the answer, but there are some indications that it may be so.

Reporting the 1936 Peking International Dog Show, which took

Bjorneholms Pysse, owned by Anita Berggren of Sweden.

Agnes van Panthaleon Baroness van Eck of the Netherlands with her British-bred Shih Tzu, Rockafella of Bracewell and Emma of Myarlune. They are pictured at the Brussells International show.

place on May 16th, by a strange mistake the *Peiping Chronicle* described it as the "Second" of its kind. "Exceptionally good were the Lhassa Lion dogs," the paper announced next day, "some excellent specimens being exhibited. This class was judged by Madame Lu, an expert and breeder of long standing and author of the book on Lhassa Lion dogs."

At this show, which was attended by the Mayor of the city and by the United States Ambassador to China, Mr. Nelson T. Johnson, "Mayflower Gaston," a dog owned by an American, Mrs. Paul Jernigan, "copped the blue ribbon for this class (the Lhasas), whilst "Biscotte," owned by the Countess d'Anjou was judged the best Lhassa Lion bitch in the show."

With a Chinese judge, for the first time on record Shih Tzu owned by foreigners were given top placings, which was either an exercise in international courtesy or a mark of increasingly responsible western involvement in the breed. There was, in fact, no mention of any Lhasa shown by a Chinese. For the first time, also, the Countess d'Anjou is mentioned as an exhibitor, and a highly successful one too, interestingly enough just seven months after the arrival in Peking of the romantic Chinese Princess from whom she learned so much about the palace dogs.

Although her lion dogs had been highly praised at the show of June, 1935, no mention of Madame Wilden's name occurs in connection with that of 1936. This is understandable, as her husband had died very suddenly of a heart attack on September 23rd, 1935, just ten days before the return to Peking of the Princess Der Ling.

By the fourth annual show in 1937 the Countess d'Anjou had clearly emerged as the leading Shih Tzu breeder in Peking, her successes being recorded in the *North China Star* of Tientsin on May 17th, 1937. This show is the last I have been able to trace and was quite possibly the last to be held. The Countess' Lhasa Lions

Norwegian Ch. Chang-Ming, owned by Tor Otto Winjusveen relaxing on the show bench with a young guest.

Mrs. L. G. Widdrington, "the lady of Lhakang," in the conservatory at Newton Hall. With her are Chs. Maya Wong and Mao Mao of Lhakang and, at the right, Shih Tipsee of Elfann. The dog being carried is Min Yuenne of Elfann.

"Nuisance" and "Hutze" took first and second places in the breed, while her "Lhassa Lion" was Best Non-Sporting bitch. At the same time her brace, "Shih Tse" and "Nuisance," were placed second in the "Small Breeds," apparently the nearest equivalent to a Toy Group. "Shih Tse" was also best bitch in show.

Looking over the four Peking Shows it is clear that the lack of effective control over the previous 20 years had led to some confusion regarding the breed in the 1930s. Some Peking fanciers were obviously doing their best to restore to the Shih Tzu something of the Imperial grandeur which had been its birthright in happier days, and the Countess d'Anjou—advised by the Princess Der Ling—was increasingly becoming the leader of this group. Unfortunately the Japanese occupation of Peking in the early summer of 1937, to be followed by Pearl Harbor $4\frac{1}{2}$ years later, brought a speedy end to their short-lived hopes and dreams.

A HIGHLY IMPORTANT DOCUMENT

Some exceptionally valuable information regarding Shih Tzu size and weight comes to us in the form of a personal letter, dated

A gathering of Shih Tzu fanciers at the Scottish Kennel Club show in Edinburgh, 1957. They are (l. to r.) Mrs. Murray-Kerr with her Ch. Ta-To of Lhakang, Mrs. L. G. Widdrington with Lhakang Mimosa of Northallerton, Mrs. Sommerfield, Mrs. Arnott with Kosi of Lhakang, and Miss and Mrs. Ross with two of their "Kashmoors."

May 1955, written by the Countess d'Anjou to Mrs. L. G. Widdrington, leading English fancier and widely recognized authority on palace lion dog history. Written by the Countess on her return to France after a visit to England, this highly important document has not yet received the attention it deserves. The contents of the letter, in entirety, will be found in the American *Shih Tzu News* of March, 1967.

The Countess begins, "I am enclosing the Standard we have made out for France." This Standard set weight limits for the Shih Tzu of 11–22 pounds, 11–15 pounds being declared preferable (*"de 5 a 10 kilogs mais de preference de 5 a 7 kilogs,"* is the exact wording), and is said to have been very carefully prepared, *"minutieusement etabli,"* by the Count and Countess d'Anjou.

The whole standard is also said to have met with the complete approval of two other French fanciers from pre-Pearl Harbor Peking, although it is highly unlikely that either of them knew nearly as much about the breed's history as the Countess. The available evidence regarding both suggests strongly that their experience of Shih Tzu dates from the confused period *before* the Princess Der

Int. and Norwegian Ch. Ack Lhe. This dog traces directly back to the original Scandinavian imports from China of 1932.

Swedish Ch. Jungfaltets Jung-Wu-Pi, an eleven-pound gold and white bitch bred and owned by Mr. and Mrs. Carl-Olof Jungefeldt. A frequent winner, she was Best Toy at the Swedish Kennel Club International show in Stockholm, May 1963, under judge Mr. Tore Edmund.

Ling arrived in Peking to bring to light the full truth about the imperial lion dogs as she had known them in the palace.

Making no reference whatsoever to the new French Standard she was enclosing, other than the eleven words just quoted, in the remainder of her letter the Countess went on to make it quite clear that she was far from happy about the weight limits permitted by it. Apparently she had accepted them against her better judgement, perhaps persuaded by her husband that they were the best possible under the conditions then prevailing in France, but very obviously she did not regard such a weight range as historically correct or even as desirable.

French Ch. Jungfaltets Jung-Wu, bred in Sweden by Mr. and Mrs. Carl-Olof Jungefeldt and owned by the late Ingrid Colwell.

The Countess's letter to Mrs. Widdrington runs, "Yes, I did think the Shih Tzu too big in England. They really should be under 12 pounds. In fact we had two classes in Peking, up to 12 pounds and over 12 pounds were judged separately. They never had the big ones in the Imperial Palace . . ."

Contrasting sharply with the much higher weight range in the Standard she was enclosing, these emphatic personal words, in her own handwriting, must surely be taken as expressing the Countess' true feelings on the subject. It must not be forgotten that her information came from the Princess Der Ling who, as a lady-in-waiting at court, had been in a unique position to know what the palace dogs were like. The Countess may well have been the only westerner to whom the facts of Shih Tzu history were made known.

The reference to two classes in Peking can only refer to a practice which must have been established by the Peking Kennel Club which

At the right is a headstudy of the Finnish and Norwegian Ch. Marinas Muff-Lung-Feng. This dog was Reserve Best in Show at Helsinki in 1968. Below is the International and Scandinavian Ch. Beldams Fu-Mao-Thing, owned by Mrs. Marianne Berg of Sweden, and bred by Beldams Kennels. The first Swedish-born International Champion in the breed, she is the dam of seven Champions including two International Champions and one Best in Show winner.

initiated dog shows in 1934 and set up a Standard for the Shih Tzu in 1938. With a weight range of 10–15 pounds, this Standard makes no mention of a division at 12 pounds, so we are fortunate to have this clearly documented evidence from the Countess that such a division into two weight classes was made in Peking. This may explain why the Countess' dogs appeared in both the "Non-Sporting" and in the "Small Breeds" at the 1937 Peking Kennel Club Show, "Lhassa Lion" in the one, "Shih Tse" and "Nuisance" in the other.

It is to be regretted that the Countess' letter gives no indication what happened to the larger Shih Tzu which must have appeared, at least occasionally, even during the days of carefully controlled

Mr. Tor Otto Winjusveen with his Ch. Chang-Ming and Mrs. Ruth Laakso and her Ch. Muff-Lung-Feng, two well-known Norwegian fanciers and their winning Shih Tzu.

court breeding. Quite possibly the Princess Der Ling was unaware of their fate and may not even have known of their existence, such matters having in all probability having been kept to themselves by the eunuchs.

An interesting suggestion is that they may have been used as fighting dogs to provide back-kitchen "sport" for the imperial servants, unknown to their royal masters and mistresses. I wrote

This scene of Shih Tzu judging was taken at the Zuidlaren International show, the Netherlands, May 1969. The dog on the table is Oko Shu van de Oranje Manege and is being handled by Miss Eta Pauptit. The dog on the ground is Ch. Ollo v. Tschomo-Lungma with Mrs. Erika Geusendam. The judge here is Mrs. Schoor.

of this in my Shih Tzu column in *Popular Dogs* magazine in October and November, 1968. Alternatively, they may have been smuggled out of the palace for sale elsewhere. Although the punishment for this is said to have been drastic, at least in theory, undoubtedly the wily eunuchs had their own ways of avoiding detection.

Stealing by the eunuchs seems to have been "taken for granted," according to Sir Reginald Johnston, and was by no means always punished on detection. Since it would have involved acknowledgement of the theft, such punishment would have meant "loss of

Miss Eta Pauptit, world-renowned breeder or Shih Tzu with two of her "Oranje Manege" yearlings at home in the Netherlands. Miss Pauptit made extensive studies of the Shih Tzu in Britain, Sweden and the United States before embarking on her breeding program. Proof of the effectiveness of her breeding efforts is shown in the numerous winners and producers all over the world that bear her illustrious kennel name.

face" for the master or mistress of the unfaithful servant. For that reason many offenses were overlooked.

Writing about his experiences in Peking in 1923, Harry A. Franke affirms that for many decades past—not least during the days of imperial rule—there had been very little effective control over the activities of the eunuchs who were virtualy a law unto themselves. We may be quite sure that they did their best to profit from all dogs of their breeding, even if it meant illicitly permitting over-size specimens to pass into the hands of the general public. This would readily explain why, when looking for Shih Tzu in Peking, the first English importers found that "some were very large."

What the Countess d'Anjou's highly important letter does make unmistakably clear is her conviction that only the smaller Shih Tzu were kept in the Imperial Palace, and her pride in the fact that some measure of priority was given to them at Peking Kennel Club Shows —an arrangement which she would very obviously have liked to see

International and Dutch Ch. Hang Shu v.d. Oranje Manege, owned and bred by Miss Eta Pauptit, is a valuable asset to his owner's stud force and breeding program. He earned his title in the strongest kind of competition and is considered a top specimen of the smaller type.

continued in Europe. In this regard the documentary evidence is beyond dispute, and it is worth recalling that the Countess is widely accepted as the leading western authority on the breed.

MORE RECENT DEVELOPMENTS IN EUROPE

As the curtain falls so dramatically on Shih Tzu history in China the scene shifts to Europe where—as we have seen—specimens of the breed were taken to the British Isles and to Scandinavia in the early 1930s.

In Scandinavia the Shih Tzu has always been recognized as small, 9–11 pounds being regarded as the desirable weight. This information comes from Mr. Carl-Olof Jungefeldt, member of the board of the Swedish Kennel Club and of the Special Club for Non-Sporting Dogs and Toys, whose success in breeding high quality Shih Tzu has been marked by the award of the important Hamilton Trophy by the Swedish Kennel Club.

Min Yuenne of Elfann, owned by Mrs. L. G. Widdrington, was one of the first of the smaller type to appear in English stock. This lovely 9½-pound black and white bitch made a valuable contribution to the breed by herself and through her descendants by helping to counteract the tendency of British Shih Tzu to be too big and coarse.

Ch. Zizi's Tara at her first show. At the tender age of ten months this lovely Norwegian homebred had the distinction of being named best in the Toy Group at the Oslo show. She is owned by Mrs. Ruth Laakso.

The Norwegian-bred bitch Marinas Dog-Rose, owned by Mrs. Ruth Laakso, is pictured here as an eleven-month-old puppy at the Jonkoping, Sweden show.

Chin Yutang of Flinthaug, owned by Mrs. Marie Hynaas of Norway.

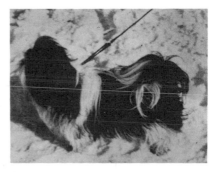

Pointing out that the breed has always been placed in the Toy group in Scandinavia, although the Standard makes no mention of weight, in his letters to me Mr. Jungefeldt emphasizes that all Swedish Shih Tzu which have won Best in Show at major events have weighed about 10 pounds.

Expressing a somewhat similar point of view, in the June, 1966, issue of the *Manchu Shih Tzu Society News Letter*, Miss Eta Pauptit, leading Dutch fancier, stresses that in five years breeding she "has never had a puppy go over 12 pounds, adult weight."

In England a different situation developed as the Shih Tzu put on weight after importation in 1930, each generation tending to grow larger than the one before. "Climatic conditions" have been suggested as a reason for this, but such an explanation fails to account

International and German Ch. Flying Tzi van Klein Vossenborg, owned by Mrs.
J. G. Lammers and bred by H. v.d. Spek. This dog is of pure Scandinavian breeding, and is totally unrelated to any of the dogs involved in the 1952 Pekingese cross.

for the fact that the Scandinavian imports and their successors appear to have remained more or less stable in size. It is much more likely that the growth in size of the English dogs reflects the fact that they were descended from larger Shih Tzu, sold by the eunuchs outside the palace.

The growth in size became more and more difficult to counteract, although stress was laid on the need to keep the breed small, since shortage of numbers mean that "in these days it was necessary to breed from every bitch we had, to keep the breed going." Details regarding this dilemma, which was to have such far-reaching effects on the future of the Shih Tzu in England, will be found in *The Manchu Shih Tzu Society, Selected Items from 1960–1963, News Letters Nos. IX-XXIV.*

Little guidance was available from China at this time, as there was still uncertainty in both Peking and Shanghai regarding the desirable size for the breed. As we have seen, it was not until October,

1935, that the Princess Der Ling arrived in Peking and was able to clarify the situation. Even so, it was only in 1938 that the Peking Kennel Club Standard for the Shih Tzu was promulgated officially.

Some assistance might have been obtained from Scandinavia, but it does not seem to have occurred to English fanciers of the 1930s to look in that direction for more knowledge of the Shih Tzu. Even today it is highly questionable whether they realize the importance of Mr. Henrik Kauffman's imports. Of two booklets on the breed prepared in recent years by English writers, one makes no suggestion whatever that any Shih Tzu reached the western world other than those brought to England, while the other refers only in the most perfunctory fashion to the existence of the Scandinavian line.

In the resulting confusion the first British standard of 1934 initially did not specify either size or weight, merely stating, "considerable variation permissible, provided other proportions are correct and true to type." Not until later were the weight limits set at 14–19 pounds, based on the size of the Shih Tzu appearing in the English rings at the time, not—as in Peking—on a study of the breed's back-

Four direct descendants of the first imports to Scandinavia: (l. to r.) Beldams E-Thing, her grandmother Swedish Ch. Beldams Ama-la-Thing, International and Norwegian Ch. Beldams Fu-Mao-Thing and their mother, Swedish and Finnish Ch. Thing-e-Ling av Brogyllen.

This gathering of English fanciers took place at the 1954 Leicester show. At the extreme left is the late Lady Brownrigg with Ch. Wang-Po of Taishan, next to her is Mrs. L. G. Widdrington with Ch. Maya Wong of Lhakang. At the right are Tony and Soo Dobson. He has an Elfann bitch and she holds Pei-Ho of Taishan later to become a Champion in Australia.

Miss Emery (left) and Lady Brownrigg with a group of the latter's early Shih Tzu. The Chinese import Shu-Ssa is second from the left, Lung-Yu is third from the right and Yangtse of Taishan is being held up by Lady Brownrigg.

ground and history. These weight limits, determined solely by the size of the few Shih Tzu then in Great Britain, remained in force, until 1958.

Thus for over twenty years British Shih Tzu breeders worked with a *minimum* weight which was two pounds heavier than the *maximum* said by the Countess to have been regarded as desirable for palace dogs. They had no means of knowing this, of course, as the facts of the breed's history only gradually became known, particularly since communications must have been seriously hampered by the Japanese advance of 1937 and the subsequent harassment of westerners in North China.

In the trying war years that all too soon followed, Shih Tzu fanciers everywhere had more serious matters to occupy their attention than the setting of the correct Standard for the breed. Not surprisingly, it seems to have been a very considerable time before English breeders fully realized that the Peking Kennel Club had set a Standard with weight limits very different from their own.

Mrs. L. G. Widdrington and her daughter Christie photographed in 1946 with Mee Na of Taishan, the foundation bitch of the Lhakang line. Mee Na was bred by the Brownriggs. Sire: Yangtse of Taishan; dam: Tzu-Hsi. The puppies here were out of Mee Na by Ch. Choo-Ling, a grandson of the Royal Family's well-known Choo-Choo.

Chumulari Huo-Chi, **owned by** Mrs. Clara Bothe. **This engaging seven-month-old bitch is of the typical gold-and-white color.**

Perhaps even more disconcerting must have been the fact that, "on numerous occasions visitors from China who came to see us at shows would tell us: 'Your dogs are very lovely, but far too big'." Hearing such criticism repeatedly from those who obviously knew what they were talking about, it is little wonder that conscientious fanciers found themselves compelled to recognize that "things were not really right with the breed."

It is understandable that, not long after the Countess d'Anjou's letter to Mrs. Widdrington had made the position crystal clear, Mr. K. B. Rawlings, Chairman of the British Shih Tzu Club, should have explained at the Club's Annual General Meeting that some change in weight range must be made. "Over the years the breed has been getting far too large," Mr. Rawlings admitted frankly, when questioned.

An illuminating hindsight on this situation is found in the cautionary phrase in the present British Standard, "type and breed characteristics of the utmost importance and on no account to be sacrificed

A group of the famous Lhakang Shih Tzu relaxing with their owner Mrs. L. G. Widdrington at Newton Hall, Northumberland, England.

to size alone." While no one will quarrel with such a praise-worthy expression of opinion, it is highly significant that nothing of this nature appears in the Peking Kennel Club Standard. Strongly defensive in tone, these words would appear to have been inserted by British breeders to explain and justify their use of larger dogs when they had no other choice.

Much the same might be said of the oft-quoted assertion from the British Standard that the Shih Tzu is "neither a terrier nor a toy," an essentially negative and defensive statement to which I have as yet found no parallel in Peking Kennel Club writings and with which Scandinavian breeders could hardly be expected to agree.

It is certainly not true in the United States, where the American Kennel Club has placed the Shih Tzu in the Toy Group, a decision which was strongly resisted by a few breeders but which the vast majority have accepted gladly.

In the movement to lower the weight limits set by the first British Standard, a leading part was taken by Mrs. L. G. Widdrington, President of the Manchu Shih Tzu Society, who has done much

Ch. Mao Mao of Lhakang with her daughters Kosi and the future Champion Maya Wong of Lhakang.

Lhakang Mimosa of Northallerton with Miss Christie Widdrington. Mimosa has been described as one of the best of the gold-colored Shih Tzu to be seen in Britain. This bitch has also produced golden puppies thereby introducing this badly needed color phase to Britain.

for the betterment of the breed in Great Britain and beyond.

"As regards my own breeding operations, although I had bred Shih Tzu upwards of fifteen years, and many had become Champions, they were all bigger than they should be, and there seemed nowhere to turn to stop a continuous upward trend," Mrs. Widdrington writes, recalling her early frustrations, "I often used to think 'How gorgeous this or that one would be if only half the size' but there seemed at the time little hope of establishing the breed in the size it should be, i.e. under 12 pounds. Even by using the smallest good dog available, the offspring were often larger than either parent."

In these early days, Mrs. Widdrington recalls regretfully, an Anglo-Chinese lady, resident in England, booked two bitch puppies from her before seeing any English Shih Tzu. Visiting a major English show before taking delivery, she promptly cancelled the order, disappointed at the size of the exhibited and insisting that the true Shih Tzu should be "small and jewel-like."

In 1954 it was discovered, by happy chance, that the union of certain bloodlines made it possible to reduce the size of the British strain. This led to the formation of the Manchu Shih Tzu Society, originally founded "to promote and protect the interests of the smaller Shih Tzu (12 pounds and under) as bred in the Imperial Palace, Peking." Now by far the larger of the two clubs in Great Britain devoted to the Shih Tzu, in 1968 the Manchu Shih Tzu Society had 283 members, the British Shih Tzu Club 166.

Encouraging the appearance of smaller Shih Tzu in the show ring, the Manchu Shih Tzu Society founders drew renewed public attention to the breed. So popular did they become that within a short space of time it was estimated that at least half of those registered with the British Kennel Club were of the smaller type.

"Since the smaller dogs have appeared at shows, people who knew the breed in China have hailed them as being more correct in size and type, and judges who remember the original dogs have put them up," Mrs. Widdrington recalls thoughtfully.

"In 1957, after dining at the Palace Hotel, Paignton, after the show, some of us were strolling round the gardens with our dogs, when a distinguished-looking elderly lady came running breathlessly after us, explaining she had owned similar dogs in China. Her husband came running from the car and both were thrilled and filled with nostalgic memories to come across the breed over here," Mrs.

Widdrington continues, "She looked over my little Min Yuenne and Tien Memsahib carefully, both black-and-white and not more than 10 pounds, and pronounced them identical in size and coloring to the ones she had owned in China."

While in Peking, General Sir Douglas Brownrigg had been Assistant Adjutant and Quartermaster General to the British Army's North China Command. Some years after his return to England he was appointed an aide-de-camp to King George V, a position which he occupied from 1933 to 1934. During these early years he and Lady Brownrigg took a leading part in introducing the new breed to the English public.

We are told that Lady Brownrigg was very particular about keeping the noses short and that she would go round the benches at shows, measuring each exhibit with the end joint of her thumb to make sure that none were over an inch in length. "She also constantly warned against letting the breed get too big," recalls Mrs. Widdrington in

Jen-Kai-Ko of Lhakang, owned by Mr. and Mrs. A. Fox and bred by Mrs. L. G. Widdrington. At this writing the holder of two Challenge Certificates, "Chunky" has gone Best in Show twice and has numerous Best of Breed wins to his credit. Through his sire he traces back to the Jungfaltets line of Sweden, and through his dam his ancestry goes back to the 1949 Chinese imports Wuffles and Mai-Ting.

the April, 1969, *Manchu Shih Tzu Society News Letter*, "a tendency which the English climate seemed to encourage. Then some of the later imports, although bringing in much new blood, were inclined to throw a proportion of offspring rangier and longer-nosed than was typical."

Mrs. Widdrington gives a vivid account of her own introduction to the Shih Tzu in 1939:—

"My first glimpse of the breed was in Thurloe Square Gardens, London, on a very windy day, when Mrs. Doig, the Brownrigg's cook, was exercising about eight of them on leashes, and I thought I had never seen such amazing creatures—part lions, part Chinese dragons, part gargoyles, and I felt I MUST own one!

"I called on the Brownriggs at 48 Thurloe Square and met Mona (Lady Brownrigg) looking very charming in her Red Cross uniform. The house seemed a fitting background for these oriental dogs, being full of Chinese antiques and pictures.

The late Lady Brownrigg pictured in 1949 with Pu-Yi of Taishan. A stickler for short noses, Lady Brownrigg insisted on this in her own "Taishans". She was also one of the champions of divided classes based on weight for Shih Tzu classes in Great Britain.

A class of bitches lined up for the final selection at the Sydney Royal show, Sydney, Australia, Easter 1967.

"I was told that there was one puppy bitch left which I could have quite reasonably as it was rather big, and Lady Brownrigg was so busy just now with her Red Cross work. But I could only have her on condition that I bred and showed her. Neither had entered my mind. However, it was a promise made, and whole new worlds opened for me in the keeping of it."

The confusion of these years, made much worse by wartime difficulties, are colorfully illustrated by Mrs. Widdrington's description of a visit she and Lady Brownrigg paid to a lady in the Isle of Wight—

"A beautiful small golden 'Shih Tzu' with black tips ran joyfully to greet us, and we both pronounced it a beautiful specimen in every way. Imagine Mona's consternation when told by the owner that it wasn't a Shih Tzu at all—not a drop—but a cross between a Maltese and a Pekingese!"

General Brownrigg died with tragic suddenness in 1946, Lady Brownrigg in April, 1969, just two days after hearing the good news

French Ch. Jungfaltets Jung-Wu **(left) and** her son, owned by the late Ingrid Colwell. This photograph was found **among Mrs.** Colwell's papers after her death.

Chumulari Dorje, owned and bred by Rev. and Mrs. D. Allan Easton. Sire: Jung-faltets Wu-Po; dam: Chumulari Trari. Dorje's sire was bred by Mr. and Mrs. Carl-Olof Jungefeldt and was imported into the United States by the late Mrs. Ingrid Colwell.

of the breed's acceptance by the American Kennel Club. A devoted lover of the Shih Tzu and one of its most enthusiastic supporters, it was said of Lady Brownrigg that "she always felt that the breed needed to be kept as house pets with plenty of human companionship and she hated to think of anyone breeding them for purely commercial reasons."

British breeders finally agreed to compromise, four years after the foundation of the Manchu Shih Tzu Society, making provision for fanciers of both large and small types. This explains the change in weight limits, found in the 1958 British Standard, which were altered to include all sizes from 9 to 18 pounds. At the same time the hope was expressed that, "in a few years", the upper limit might be reduced to 16 pounds—and in time the whole weight range perhaps narrowed to 10–15 pounds, as in the Peking Kennel Club Standard.

International, German and Swiss Ch. Tang La v. Tschomo-Lungma, owned and bred by Mrs. Erika Geusendam. Tang La is a litter sister to Swiss, Czechoslovakian and Canadian Ch. Tangra v. Tschomo-Lungma, owned by Rev. and Mrs. D. Allan Easton.

Ch. Chumulari Ying-Ying, owned by Rev. and Mrs. D. Allan Easton was first in the Non-Sporting group at the United Kennel Club (Montreal) under judge James W. Trullinger. Ying was owner handled to this win by Mrs. Margaret Easton.

These changes have not yet been made, and the British Standard remains, "Up to 18 pounds. Ideal weight 9–16 pounds," the 16 pounds "ideal" maximum being stressed in the hope of getting, in the words of Mr. Rawlings, "a much better compact dog."

SOME CRITICS OF THE BRITISH STANDARD

Aimed at satisfying breeders with widely different ideas of ideal Shih Tzu size, the 1958 British Standard is a compromise. As such it has not been universally accepted as the proper solution to the complex situation arising from the course of the breed's history in that country.

Unwilling to accept even a division into two weight classes, which "merely suggest that there are two types and the judge can choose whichever he likes," the late Mr. Leo Wilson, distinguished editor of the British *Dog World*, and an all-round judge, insisted that "the judge must be educated into realising that the smaller Shih Tzu is the most typical."

"A Shih Tzu," he wrote, "should be small, yet solid, low to the ground with a short face. Grow him to outsize and he has only to fail a little in shortness of nose to be mistaken for a Lhasa Apso."

"Who wants a Shih Tzu—or any other toy breed for that matter —weighing over 14 pounds?" Mr. Wilson added, "That is bigger than many Terriers, and what need is there for such size? And don't point out to me that the breed is not a Toy. I know it is not classified as such by the Kennel Club, and that the Shih Tzu Club has gone out

The eyes are one of the most important features of a good Shih Tzu. They should be round, dark and full of expression. Any showing of white is considered a fault and is to be avoided. White will often show in the corner of the eye and this fault is common. The whole eye should fill the socket.

Chumulari Yu-Lo, owned by Mrs. Margaret Easton and John Marsh with whom she is shown here. Yu-Lo is a gold and white with black tippings.

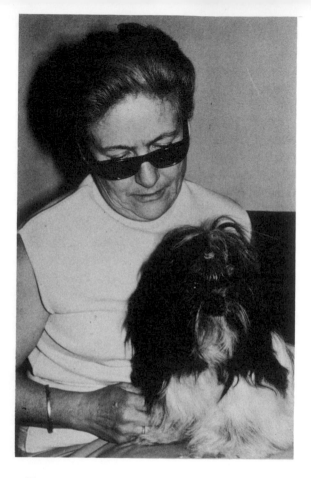

Mrs. Erika
Geusendam,
celebrated West
German Shih Tzu
breeder, with an
eight-month-old
hopeful Naga v.
Tschomo-Lungma.

of its way to point out that it is not a Toy, but that does not alter the
fact that originally the Shih Tzu was a pet, a lady's companion. And
what lady of quality in Tibet would like twenty pounds of dog flesh
on her lap?"

Mr. Wilson was understandably confused regarding the racial
origin of the old-time Shih Tzu fanciers in the Peking Palace, which
was Manchu and not Tibetan, but that does not weaken the force
of his contention that the imperial lion dogs were small. While it
may be debated whether or not they should be regarded as lap dogs,
as we have seen the fact of their smallness of size has been demonstrated beyond doubt. Mr. Wilson urged English fanciers to recognize such facts in order to avoid "a path towards a confusion which
can only be the downfall of a breed."

148

Pointing out that the smaller Shih Tzu had been proven by that time to be in the majority in England, the well-known editor and judge suggested that it was not fair that they should be shown along with the large which did not require the same carefully selective breeding.

"It is, of course, easier to breed a good big one than a good little one in any small or medium breed," he wrote, "for with size often goes coat, bone, substance of body and skull and so forth, but one might as well give Championship Certificates to Shetland Sheepdogs of 20 inches in height because they have big coats or long heads." All the above quotations are from the British *Dog World* of July 26th, 1957, page 1216.

A week later Mr. Wilson returned to the subject on which he obviously had strong feelings—

"I think it ought to be made clear," he commented vigorously, "that in talking about Shih Tzu I am just as much against weeds as I am against out-size specimens. The ideal to aim at is in my opinion

Norwegian and Danish Ch. Bjorneholms Ang Lahmu, owned by Mrs. Margit Hoffgaard of Norway and bred by Miss Astrid Jeppesen of Denmark.

The late Mrs. Ingrid Colwell with some of her Scandinavian-line Shih Tzu. Mrs. Colwell was born in Sweden and came to the United States as the bride of an American airman. Before her death in 1968 as the result of a fire, she bred many superb animals under the "Si-Kiang" prefix.

between 10 and 12 pounds, which is the happy mean." This followed in the British *Dog World* issue of August 2nd, 1957.

Similarly strong views have been expressed by Mr. Leo Helbig, international judge and highly respected leader in German dog circles, who has asserted emphatically, "breeders should have stayed with the rules, set by the Royal Palace in Peking, to breed only with dogs under 12 English pounds or 5400 grams. It would have saved a lot of headaches." The full text will be found in the German magazine, *die Hundewelt*, of April-May, 1965.

As a former resident of Peking, where I spent two happy and eventful years, I have the utmost sympathy for a point of view which must be strongly appealing to anyone who has lived long enough in the exquisite Chinese capital to appreciate the infinitely painstaking concern for detail which is one of the outstanding characteristics of so many of its artistic masterpieces.

Having also visited the harsh and rugged land of Tibet, I have no difficulty in understanding why the court breeders felt that dogs with such a background must be modified and refined in order to be suitable for the smoother and gentler environment of the Peking Palace.

Mrs. Else Grum, wife of the Danish Consul in Oslo during the 1930's. With her are Toddie, Galloping and Ting-a-Ling, three of the first Shih Tzu bred in Europe from the Kauffmann's Chinese imports.

At the same time I find myself compelled to recognize that the suggestion of Mr. Wilson, and of Mr. Helbig, does not do justice to the facts of Shih Tzu history, especially in England, and that it is not wholly fair to all present-day breeders.

Whether we like it or not, at first unwittingly and by force of circumstances rather than by deliberate choice, for nearly forty years the British Standard has permitted fanciers in that country to breed Shih Tzu well over the size which we now know was approved in the Peking Imperial Palace.

Even now that the facts regarding the breed's background and history are more fully known, it appears that there are some English breeders who still prefer to breed dogs of the larger type. We can well understand their feelings in this regard, since it is natural that they should have become attached to the dogs which they have been permitted to breed in England for so many years.

For these reasons, quite irrespective of my own personal preference, I believe that it would be wholly wrong, at this late stage, to suggest that the British Standard be altered to deprive breeders of that country of their long-standing right to breed the larger type of Shih Tzu.

Miss Astrid Jeppesen of Denmark with a group of her world-famous Bjorneholms Shih Tzu.

Ch. Chumulari Hih-Hih, owned by Richard Bauer and bred by Rev. and Mrs. D. Allan Easton. Hih-Hih is an exquisite deep gold color and has a black mask. While the breed was in the Miscellaneous class she was the top winning Shih Tzu of 1967 and 1968.

With his flowing beauty and audacious manner the Shih Tzu makes the ideal show dog. Those who have the pleasure of exhibiting him in the ring appreciate what an aristocrat the Shih Tzu is among show dogs.

Chumulari Erh-Tzu-Ying, owned by Mrs. Glae S. Bickford.

This also applies to the United States and other countries where it is essential that fair consideration should be given to those who, having at the time no means of knowing the full details of the breed's story, have in good faith imported, or bred, dogs of the larger type.

In addition, like the palace servants every Shih Tzu breeder is liable at some time to find himself with one or two larger specimens in a litter that is otherwise small. While some—like myself—would not wish such dogs of their breeding to appear in the show ring, it would be highly unrealistic to suggest that this feeling would be shared by more than a tiny minority of very strictly selective breeders. Nor is there any reason why it should be, since we do recognize that there were larger specimens in Peking, although they were not kept in the palace.

The only fair solution, in my opinion, is that we should follow the example set by the Peking Kennel Club when it was discovered that, even in the breed's native city, a considerable variation in size had developed in the years following the break-down of restricted court breeding. Such a solution involves a division which frankly recognizes the co-existence of two types of Shih Tzu, small and large, but—if the Countess d'Anjou is to be believed—gives a measure of priority to the smaller as representing the imperial ideal.

Some slight hint of this is to be found in an article by Mr. Will C. Mooney, long-time American fancier, who wrote in the American *Dog World* magazine in December, 1964:

"There are two distinct sizes of these dogs, the smaller dogs being from 8 to 10 pounds, the larger members of the breed scaling around 18 to 20 pounds. However, although two distinctly different sizes are recognized, the breed is not separated into different varieties, as are some breeds of dogs."

Some months later a leading English breeder,. Mrs. Marion C. Boot, added with even more vigor:

"If we are wanting to make changes why don't the two clubs (the Manchu Society and the Shih Tzu Club iron out the problem of the two wide-apart sizes as there is no comparison at all between a nine pounder and an eighteen pounder." This was in the British *Dog World* of April 1st, 1966, on page 614.

Attempts to establish some such division had been made before at a much earlier date by other well-known English fanciers. At the 1956 annual general meeting of the British Shih Tzu Club Mrs. L. G. Widdrington, seconded by Mrs. Audrey Fowler, moved that "classes for Shih Tzu under 12 pounds weight (adult) be put on at two or more shows in 1956." When this motion was defeated by one vote (9–10, with 2 abstentions), Mrs. Widdrington and Mrs. Fowler went on to move and second that "a separate club be formed" to further the interests of those desirous of breeding the smaller type of Shih Tzu.

"Further discussion regarding the advisability of the Club altering its present policy in order to support the breeding and showing of two sizes in the breed ensued."

The motion to form a separate club was lost by four votes (7–11,

Lady Haggerston with Ch. Sherez of Ellingham, Darzee of Clystvale and Michel-combe Chrystal of Clystvale. An American by birth, Lady Haggerston's permanent home is in Great Britain, and she is an enthusiastic supporter of the breed in her adopted country.

It is a healthy situation when fanciers endeavor to learn about a breed that is new to most of them. Such an educational session is taking place here under the auspices of the Progressive Dog Club, an organization composed of Toy breed enthusiasts. Mrs. Margaret Easton is explaining the fine points of Shih Tzu conformation to Mrs. E. R. Blamey, a well-known Pekingese fancier. The model is the puppy Chumulari Sheng-Li Che and the other dogs shown are Ch. Chumulari Ying-Ying (foreground) and Chumulari Me-Lah (partially hidden).

with 3 abstentions). The above quotations are from the minutes of the annual general meeting of the Shih Tzu Club, March 27th, 1956.

At the Shih Tzu Club's annual general meeting in the following year Lady Brownrigg returned to the subject with the proposition that the breed be divided into two sizes, up to and over 12 pounds. Mrs. Bode spoke at some length on the question, saying that there were at that time three distinct sizes and that many of the dogs were far too big.

After much all round discussion an amendment was proposed by Mrs. Rawlings, and seconded by Mrs. Leslie, that "the Standard be altered to cater for the smaller Shih Tzus, i.e. the weight for the standard size be 12 pounds to 18 pounds and for the smaller dogs, 8 to 12 pounds." This amendment was carried unanimously.

Ch. Chumulari Hih-Hih is shown here winning the Miscellaneous Class at the Mid-Hudson Kennel Club under James Trullinger in June of 1969. She was handled here by her owner Richard Bauer.

At the same meeting Mrs. Bode proposed that the Shih Tzu Club should sponsor the Imperial Palace Shih Tzu Society (the name first given to the Manchu Shih Tzu Society), the motion being seconded by Mrs. Watts-Farmer. Citing the increased number of registrations in the past year, Mrs. Bode said that these were in no small measure due to the number of breeders who "now prefer the smaller size."

The motion to sponsor the formation of such a separate club, to protect and further the interests of the smaller palace-type Shih Tzu, was carried by 12 votes to 7, with 3 abstentions. Now known as the Manchu Shih Tzu Society, this younger club—as we have seen— now has a substantially larger membership than the sponsoring body, demonstrating the widespread appeal of the palace type of dog.

All quotations with regard to this are taken from the Minutes of the Annual General Meeting of the Shih Tzu Club, held in London on March 29th, 1957.

In urging the need for a division of the Shih Tzu into two classes, we can derive immense encouragement from the fact that a precisely

Rev. and Mrs. D. Allan Easton with a group of their homebred and imported Shih Tzu.

These two puppies are typical of the best American-bred Shih Tzu. The breed in the United States has a solid background of the finest British and continental bloodlines and a following of sincere fanciers to guide the Shih Tzu's fortune in the right direction.

similar conclusion was unanimously reached by the members of the British Shih Tzu Club at the 1957 annual general meeting to which I have just referred. This meeting appears to have been attended by the vast majority of those who are now leading breeders in that country, including the key figures in both the present clubs devoted to the breed, all of whom must have given their approval to the proposal.

Such a division would undoubtedly have been made, had not the British Kennel Club taken the attitude that the breed was not sufficiently numerous to be split into two classes and that fanciers would be wiser to go ahead on a broad over-all basis, 9–18 pounds being the figure finally decided with 16 pounds the "ideal" maximum.

Written by Mr. K. B. Rawlings, then and now Chairman of the British Shih Tzu Club, an illuminating letter regarding this was published in the British *Dog World* on August 2nd, 1957. In the letter Mr. Rawlings explains that the Kennel Club was not prepared to accept the recommendations unanimously made by Club Members at the annual general meeting, either with regard to the two weight ranges or with regard to the formation of a new club to foster the smaller type of dog, and that for that reason no change could be made "until further decisions are taken by the Shih Tzu Club for submission to the Kennel Club."

In this regard it must very respectfully be suggested that the members of the British Shih Tzu Club were right in their original decision, the British Kennel Club very sadly mistaken in rejecting it. Had the Club's unanimous recommendation of 1957 been accepted by the British Kennel Club, frank recognition being given to the fact that there are now two distinctly different types of Shih Tzu, the breed would be in a much less confused state today.

That this is true of Great Britain as well as of the United States is indicated by Mrs. Marion Boot's letter, quoted earlier. Even as it is, apparently due to the pressure of obvious necessity, a division into two weight classes is being made at a number of British shows,

Two-year-old Camilla Rindmo with Ta'Hay's Puz-Puz, a five-month-old puppy bred by Mr. Caj Rindmo of Sweden.

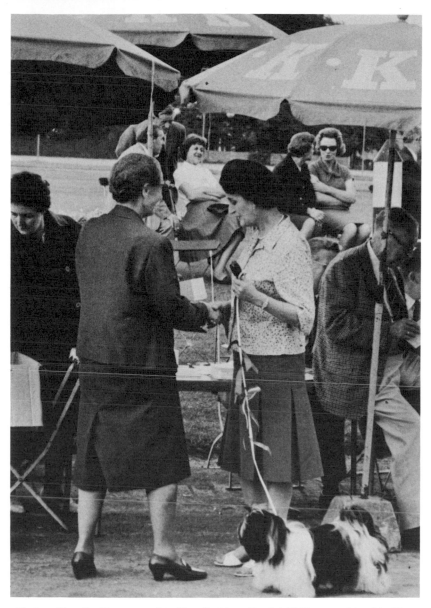

Marinas Mao Da-Ling, owned by Mrs. Kathleen Bewick-Hallberg and bred by Mrs. Marianne Berg. Shown first at the age of eight months, Da-Ling was Best of Breed and second in the Group under Mr. George Leatt of England at the Charlottenlund International Show in Denmark.

Henriette van Panthaleon Baroness van Eck with the puppy, Hwang-Han v.d. Blauwe Mammouth and his parents Giri Shu v.d. Oranje Manege (left) and Fan-Kea v.d. Blauwe Mammouth was exported to the United States to benefit the breed in his new home.

the break being made at 12 or 14 pounds—the former, of course, following the pattern set by the Peking Kennel Club whose example is only now beginning to receive the attention it deserves.

As recently as April, 1969, the American magazine *Dog World*, considered newsworthy the recognition by some breeders that "two distinct types of Shih Tzu exist—the larger, robust English Shih Tzu and the personable Scandinavian version," a very sweeping statement which completely overlooks the fact that not a few English breeders take very special pride in producing the same exquisite little gems as were favored in the Imperial Palace.

Betraying no awareness of the historical facts which lie behind the existence of the two distinct sizes, and expressing no particular interest in finding out what they were, the article indicated that such breeders planned to "combine" the best qualities of both types to produce "a new and, they hope, superior American Shih Tzu."

It is to be fervently hoped that most breeders will try to breed the best possible Chinese Shih Tzu rather than "improved" English or

If the hair on the Shih Tzu's head is allowed to hang over his eyes it will not only take away the breed's lovely expression, but can be harmful to the eyes as well. It is best to keep the hair brushed up and tied into a topknot at all times.

American versions. For this reason, breeding between the two size types should not be undertaken in a haphazard fashion but with the utmost discrimination and with a clear picture in mind of the Peking Palace prototype.

A POSSIBLE SOLUTION FROM HOLLAND

The wisdom of a weight division has been challenged on the grounds that dogs vary in weight from time to time, not to mention other practical difficulties. These have been clearly described by the British fancier, Mrs. Thelma Morgan, in the British *Dog World* of May 20th, 1966. For this reason we might do well to consider whether there is not some other more effective way of distinguishing small Shih Tzu from large.

When the Countess d'Anjou wrote her letter to Mrs. Widdrington, it must be realized that her purpose was to make it clear that the palace dogs were smaller in size than those which she had just seen in England but which she was hardly likely to have weighed. Even more important she was *not* affirming that the court in Peking had established a 12 pound limit. This becomes obvious when we recall that the avoirdupois weight system of pounds and ounces is an essentially western concept.

Mrs. Ruth Laakso with two eight-week-old puppies, Zizi's Che-La and Zizi's Kong Feng. Mrs. Laakso, a Dane living in Norway, is an enthusiastic breeder and supporter of the Shih Tzu, and many top winning continental dogs bear her well-known prefix.

Public interest in the Shih Tzu has been gathering momentum very quickly since the breed began to appear at shows. At the Rittenhouse Square Dog Show, an invitational exhibition, Ch. Chumulari Ying-Ying enjoys a quiet moment with Mrs. Margaret Easton while he represents the breed at this popular Philadelphia affair.

Thus a 12 pound weight limit would have been quite meaningless to the palace eunuchs who most certainly did not use English or American-made scales to weigh their puppies! As any "old China hand" will readily appreciate, their over-all objective was to produce the most compact dogs possible, exquisite little gems treasured for their neatness of size—not their lightness of weight.

We should recall in this regard the Empress-Dowager's own pronouncement, "Let the Lion Dog be Small," being the opening words of "Pearls Dropped from the Lips of Her Imperial Majesty Tzu Hsi, Dowager Empress of the Flowery Land of Confucius," quoted in Mrs. Dixey's *The Lion Dog of Peking*.

As a careful reading of the Countess d'Anjou's letter will show, the reference to a 12 pounds maximum occurs because the Peking Kennel Club had decided that this was the best way to separate the large dogs from the small, possibly through the influence of British or American members to whom such a measurement of weight would come naturally.

On this subject the opinion of the Peking Kennel Club deserves to be treated with the utmost respect, much more so than it has received to date in the English-speaking world. Such respect does not mean that we should follow their example blindly, however, if we can devise some better method of achieving the same objective—which, after all, is to distinguish the dainty palace-type Shih Tzu from the less compact ones which have become so frequently in evidence since the break-down of the court breeding program.

Concerning this I have received a suggestion from the Netherlands which I find of the greatest interest. Originally written to me personally, it has since appeared in the Christmas 1968 issue of the Dutch magazine, *De Hondenwereld*. A most helpful and constructive criticism of the Peking Kennel Club's mode of division, it suggests a method which could both be simpler and more satisfactory.

"I agree that we should be breeding small dogs as the Chinese undoubtedly did. However a small dog could have bone and look less heavy than he actually weighs. What makes some Shih Tzu heavy is not only bone-structure, but width of chest and length of back, the latter even giving a large impression to an otherwise small dog. Then a dog with slightly bowed forelegs will be lower at withers than one with straight legs."

"To establish a fair method of size differentiation," continues my

The Baroness Van Panthaleon Van Eck of the Netherlands with her stud dog Giri Shu v.d. Oranje Manege and the newly arrived, eight-week-old puppy Zizi's Leidza. The Baroness conceived the idea for measuring Shih Tzu in the ring as described in this text.

Hwang-Han v.d. Blauwe Mammouth, owned by Rev. and Mrs. D. Allan Easton and bred by the Baroness Van Panthaleon Van Eck of the Netherlands. This puppy was presented to the Eastons in recognition of their services on behalf of the Shih Tzu breed.

Netherlands correspondent, the Baronesse Van Panthaleon Van Eck, wife of the Burgomaster of Emmeloord and Shih Tzu columnist for *De Hondenwereld*, "measure from one forefoot over withers to the other forefoot, following the legs closely. Add the length of back from exactly between withers to beginning of tail. After some measuring I come to a maximum of 35 inches for the 'small gems.' But hundreds of dogs would have to be measured that way to fix the right size. Every judge could keep a string with a knot in it in his pocket to measure in the ring, if necessary."

Not nearly so subject to variability as weight, this highly ingenious Dutch suggestion is much less complicated than it seems on first reading. Since it makes provision for the fact that a sturdily boned and compact Shih Tzu can be surprisingly heavy, it may well provide the solution to our problem. At least it is worth the most serious

A Shih Tzu will often look larger than he really is because of the profuse coat he carries. This will apply even to puppies such as the four-month-old specimen shown here.

consideration. I might mention that the Baroness is a devoted Shih Tzu fancier, breeding selectively with a few dearly loved house-pets of the smaller type.

THE IMPERIAL SHIH TZU

After the manuscript for this book had been sent to the publisher, our continuing search for first-hand information brought to light a little-known essay by the Princess Der Ling which fully confirms the theory we have advanced regarding the development of two different types of Shih Tzu in old Peking.

Describing the royal kennels in this essay, which was published in the United States in 1933, the Princess gives some fascinating glimpses of the information which she received from the Empress Dowager about her beloved dogs.

"Out of a litter of four," Her Majesty told me, "there are seldom more than two which are worth keeping. The others, even though they have the same father and mother, have something the matter with them—too short legs, too long bodies, or the wrong markings. They are inferior."

"Particular care must be taken with feeding," explained Her Majesty. "*A Harba Go* (Manchu words for this species of dog) must not be given too much water while he is growing, or he will become too large, which makes him ugly. The food must be as carefully selected as for a child . . ."

"If Her Majesty wished to examine one of the dogs closer she would indicate which one and the eunuch would hold the animal up for her inspection. Then she would say, 'Its eyes are dirty; you must take better care of it,' or 'Its hind legs are not of the right length,' or 'Its body is too long.' Whenever she commented thus on any dog, especially the puppies, it was a decree of exile—for it meant that the dog had to be taken away. Puppies were not killed," wrote the Princess. "The eunuchs usually took discarded puppies out into the city and sold them, receiving good prices because the animals were from the imperial kennels."

Clearly it was no secret that the palace eunuchs were able to find willing purchasers for the puppies which the Empress Dowager had rejected as inferior in quality. This would seem to have been accepted as the normal practice and to have been done on a considerable scale.

Being intensely fond of animals, doubtless the strong-willed old ruler was glad to see her puppies go to homes where they were valued, even though she regarded them as poor specimens of the breed. It may well have been her hope that they would be treated as pets, not used for breeding, but this was a matter over which she had no means of exercising effective control. Indeed it is questionable how much she knew of what went on outside the palace walls, as the life of the court was completely cut off from that of the ordinary citizens of Peking.

As a result, it is easy to see how two different types of Shih Tzu had developed in the Chinese capital by the time the breed became known to the outside world. On the one hand, hidden in the palace and beloved at court were the exquisitely dainty and well-proportioned little jewels, bred with the strictest selectivity and carefully screened to conform to the imperial ideal. On the other, accessible to the general public and bred by them with less discrimination were the coarser specimens, treasured by those who had long ago learned to be satisfied with something less than the best.

Shih Tzu of both types are to be seen in the show rings of England and North America today, though much less so in continental Europe where the neat but sturdy palace variety have always been recognized as the correct imperial dogs. Generally speaking, in the West the larger and coarser dogs have lost their Oriental appearance, while the more compact and daintier ones have retained a distinctively Chinese look. Although exaggerated, there is a measure of truth in the comment of a leading European authority—with an affection for both types—who wrote, "I regard them as, more or less, different breeds."

In fairness to the general public, which does have its rights in the matter, the two types of Shih Tzu should be clearly designated in a manner which is historically accurate and in no way misleading. It had occurred to me that the larger could be known as the "English Shih Tzu," since it is in that country that most of them now seem to be bred, but such a title would obscure the fact that many English breeders prefer the smaller type. Perhaps the larger should just be known as "Shih Tzu," the smaller carrying the prefix "Imperial" to mark their special association with the Peking Palace.

It remains only to add that the Imperial Shih Tzu cannot be bred in any other way than on a very small scale and in a highly personal

Ch. Bjorneholms Pif, owned by Mariljac Kennels and bred by Miss Astrid Jeppesen of Denmark. Sire: Int. Ch. Bjorneholms Wu Ling; Dam: Ranga Ling. Pif, a 10½-pound gold and while male arrived in the United States in 1968 after being widely campaigned in Europe and annexing Championship titles in Denmark, Germany, Switzerland, Belgium and Czechoslovakia. Of pure Scandinavian bloodlines, this dog has the distinction of being the first of the breed to become a Champion in the United States.

fashion. Reared with the greatest individual care and attention by the court eunuchs, the breed has derived its unique character from its close association with the human race.

Those who think in terms of large scale breeding in kennels, with an impressive listing of studs and bitches, would be well advised to confine their attention to the larger type of Shih Tzu. The smaller ones should be left strictly to the fancier with a few dearly loved house-pets which he is content to breed in a carefully restricted and highly selective manner.

None of us can offer the Imperial Shih Tzu the pomp and glory of palace life, but—given plenty of affection and an honored place in our homes—they will be more than happy to attach themselves to the humblest family circle and to bring to it something of the splendor and dignity which is their heritage as a royal breed.

CHAPTER IV

THE SHIH TZU STANDARD

The Board of Directors of The American Kennel Club has approved the following Standard for Shih Tzu, to be effective September 1, 1969:

General Appearance: Very active, lively and alert, with a distinctly arrogant carriage. The Shih Tzu is proud of bearing as befits his noble ancestry, and walks with head well up and tail carried gaily over the back.

Head: Broad and round, wide between the eyes. Muzzle square and short, but not wrinkled, about one inch from tip of nose to stop. *Definite Stop. Eyes:* Large, dark and round but not prominent, placed well apart. Eyes should show warm expression. *Ears:* Large, with long leathers, and carried drooping; set slightly below the crown of the skull; so heavily coated that they appear to blend with the hair of the neck. *Teeth:* Level or slightly undershot bite.

Forequarters: Legs short, straight, well boned, muscular, and heavily coated. Legs and feet look massive on account of the wealth of hair.

Body: Body between the withers and the root of the tail is somewhat longer than the height at the withers; well coupled and sturdy. Chest broad and deep, shoulders firm, back level.

Hindquarters: Legs short, well boned and muscular, are straight when viewed from the rear. Thighs well rounded and muscular. Legs look massive on account of wealth of hair.

Feet: Of good size, firm, well padded, with hair between the pads. Dewclaws, if any, on the hind legs are generally removed. Dewclaws on the forelegs may be removed.

Tail: Heavily plumed and curved well over the back; carried gaily, set on high.

Coat: A luxurious, long, dense coat. May be slightly wavy but *not* curly. Good woolly undercoat. The hair on top of the head may be tied up.

Color: All colors permissible. Nose and eye rims black, except that dogs with liver markings may have liver noses and slightly lighter eyes.

SHIH TZU: DESCRIPTION AND SUGGESTED STANDARD

ORIGIN: The SHIH TZU, SHIH TZU KOU, or LION DOG, comes from Peking, China, where it was believed to have originated in the Imperial Palace as a result of selective crossbreeding between Tibetan Tribute Dogs and the native Pekingese. The breed was first brought from China to Great Britain in 1930 and to Scandinavia in 1932.

BODY: Between withers and root of tail should be longer than height at withers, but well-coupled and sturdy.

HEIGHT AT WITHERS: 8–10½ inches.

WEIGHT: Up to 15 lbs. Ideal weight 9–12 lbs. Small dogs preferred provided they have substance. The larger ones were not kept in the Imperial Palace.

COAT: Long and dense with good undercoat and may have a slight wave towards the end.

COLOR: All colors permissible. Honey and gold highly favored in Peking, being the Imperial color: also white blaze on forehead, white tip to tail, and four white feet.

TAIL: Well plumed and carried gaily over the back.

HIND-QUARTERS: Legs short, well boned and muscular. From the side they should be well angulated with good bend of stifle and hocks well let down. From the rear they should be parallel.

THIGHS: Well rounded and muscular.

APRON AND BREECHES: Well furnished and long.

NECK: Short and strong

WITHERS

HEAD AND SKULL: Broad and round: wide between the eyes. Good head furnishings essential. The hair growing upwards on the nose gives puppies a distinctively chrysanthemum-like face; in adult dogs it may be brushed up with hair on forehead to form a top-knot, held in place by an elastic band, while whiskers are trained to fall neatly on each side of the jaw

EARS: Large with long leathers and carried drooping, set slightly below the crown of skull

EYES: Dark, large clear, and round but not protruding

MUZZLE: Black, square and short, not to exceed 1 inch from tip to stop

BITE: Level or slightly undershot

WHISKERS: Long and Oriental in appearance

FORE-QUARTERS: Legs short, straight and muscular, with ample bone, firm at the shoulder

LEGS AND FEET: Should look massive on account of wealth of hair.
PAWS: Broad and firm. **GAIT:** Slightly rolling, smooth and flowing. Good reach in the forequarters and a strong rear action drive. **REAR PADS** should flash as dog moves directly away.

CHARACTERISTICS: Distinctly arrogant and aristocratic in bearing, as befits their royal background, Shih Tzu are at the same time very active and full of life. While independent in spirit they are exceptionally good-natured and affectionate, thriving on unusually close and intimate association with the human race. Reared in kennels or cages, or kept in numbers too large for intensive care and attention, they quickly lose the distinctive character and personality which gives the breed it unique charm.

Level bite

Undershot bite

Overshot bite. Faulty.

Gait: Slightly rolling, smooth and flowing, with strong rear action.

Size: Height at withers—9 to 10½ inches—should be no more than 11 inches nor less than 8 inches. Weight of mature dogs—12 to 15 pounds—should be no more than 18 pounds nor less than 9 pounds. However, type and breed characteristics are of the greatest importance.

Faults: Narrow head, overshot bite, snipiness, pink on nose or eye rims, small or light eyes, legginess, sparse coat, lack of definite stop.

This photograph shows a front view of the correct, undershot mouth. This is a characteristic many of the oriental breeds share. The Pekingese and the Lhasa Apso, the Shih Tzu's two closest relatives, both show this characteristic.

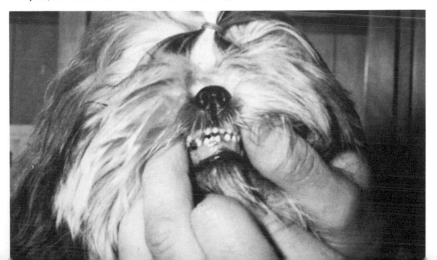

CHAPTER V

BUYING YOUR SHIH TZU PUPPY

There are several trails that will lead you to a litter of puppies where you can find the Shih Tzu of your choice. There are the classified columns in the newspaper and dog magazines. Or it is hoped that you will be able to attend a few dog shows so that you might see several specimens in the show ring. And in that way you may also contact kennel owners through the catalogue at the show or speak to the owners in person where the dogs are benched while not actually appearing in the show ring. You would also do well to write or telephone either the American Kennel Club, 51 Madison Avenue, New York, New York, 10014, or *Popular Dogs*, 2009 Ranstead Street, Philadelphia, Pa., and request the name and address of one of their reputable advertisers. These sources will put you in touch with breeders who have healthy, quality puppies for sale.

Once you have chosen the Shih Tzu as your breed because you admire its exceptional beauty, intelligence, and personality, and because you feel the Shih Tzu will fit in with your family's way of life, it is wise to speak to as many people as possible on the breed. Dog show exhibitors, the public library, the American Kennel Club library, bookshops, the clubs, can perhaps supply you with information about the breed, though most everything on the Shih Tzu that anyone need know is included in this book. One you have read everything about the breed it is time to start writing your letters and making phone calls and appointments to see puppies.

A word of caution: Don't let your choice of a kennel be determined by its nearness to your home, and then buy the first "cute" puppy that romps across your feet or licks the end of your nose! All puppies are cute, and naturally you'll have a preference among those

Shih Tzu are "people" dogs, and puppies should be handled as much as possible to encourage the development of proper disposition.

you see. But don't let preferences sway you into making the wrong decision. If you are buying your Shih Tzu as a family pet preferences are a little safer. But if you've had a color preference since you first started to consider buying a Shih Tzu, you would be wiser to stick to it—color or coat pattern is important in any breed. But if you are looking for a quality puppy with show prospects, you must think clearly, choose carefully and wisely, and make the very best possible choice. You will learn to love your Shih Tzu, whichever one you eventually choose, whereas a case of "love at first sight" can be disappointing and expensive later on if a show career has been your primary objective.

To get the broadest possible concept of what is for sale and the current market prices, it is recommended that you visit as many kennels as possible in your area and write to others farther away.

This five-month-old puppy shows the beginnings of a topknot. Later this will grow with the rest of the coat and form the "palm tree" shape which is such a typical and lovely feature of mature animals.

Quite naturally the coat grows steadily as the puppy matures. This is a photograph of Ch. Chumulari Ying-Ying at the age of ten months. At this age the dog has not yet reached the full bloom of maturity nor is the oriental look yet present. With time and careful conditioning a well-bred Shih Tzu will carry the look that endears the breed to so many.

With today's reasonably safe, inexpensive and rapid air cargo flights on the major airlines, it is possible to secure dogs from far-off places at nominal additional costs. While it is always safest to see the dog you are buying, there are enough reputable breeders and kennels to be found for you to buy a dog with a minimum of risk once you have made up your mind what you want. It can be well worth your while to obtain the exact dog or bloodline you desire if you are sincere about breeding with an eye toward improving the breed.

A SHIH TZU PUPPY GROWS UP. At the age of eight days (photo above) the eyes and ears are still closed. The white blaze on the head and the white forepaws are clearly evident and indicate that this puppy will be of a highly-prized coloring at maturity. At birth a Shih Tzu puppy weighs between two and four ounces.

The eyes and ears have now opened and are functioning normally. Even at the tender age of fourteen days the eyes are full and dark as required by the standard of the breed.

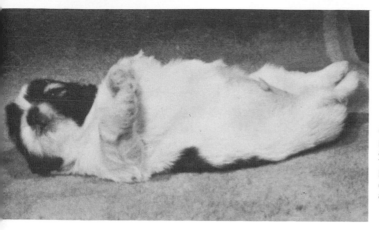

Good bone, if
present, is visible
at a very early age.
This two-weeks'
baby shows that he
displays this
attribute admirably.

The standard asks
for a broad,
rounded head, as
in this puppy.
Size and shape of
the head also
become apparent
at an early age.

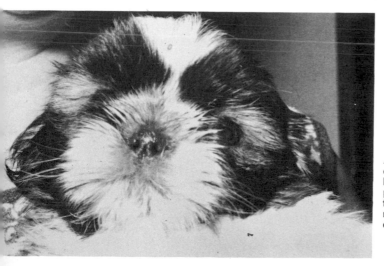

At six weeks the
coat has begun to
lengthen and the
puppy begins to
take on the
resemblance of
one of his breed.

It is customary for the purchaser to pay the shipping charges, and the airlines are most willing to supply flight information and prices upon request. Rental on the shipping crate, if the owner does not provide one for you, is usually very low. And they have now gotten them to the point of utmost safety and practicality. Barring unforeseen circumstances the safe arrival of your dog can pretty much be assured if all directions and flight plans are carefully checked out by both the buyer and the seller.

THE PUPPY YOU BUY

Let us assume you are going to buy a two- to three-month-old puppy. This is about the age when a puppy is weaned, wormed and ready to go out into the world with his new owner. Perhaps even before you notice much about his appearance you will observe his behavior. Puppies, as they are recalled in our fondest memories, are quite gay and active, as well they should be! The normal puppy should be interested, alert, and quite curious, especially about a stranger. If a puppy acts a little strange or distant, however, this need not be misconstrued as shyness or fear. He just hasn't made up his mind if he likes you. By the same token, he should not be fearful or terrified by you—and especially not by his owner!

This fine litter of seven was bred in Sweden by Mr. Caj Rindmo. Their proud dam, Larcing's Cha Cha, joins them in sitting for this engaging portrait.

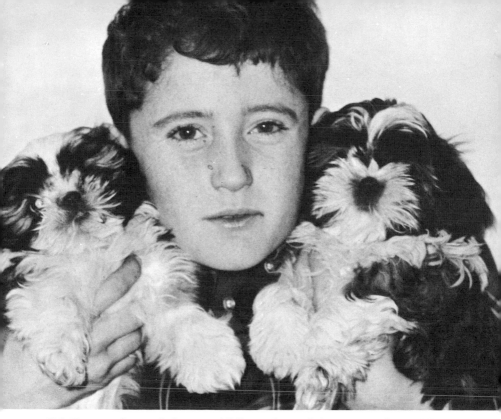

Shih Tzu are a happy choice as a child's pet due to their exceptionally good dispositions and their affinity for human companionship.

In direct contrast, the puppy should not be ridiculously over-active either. The puppy that frantically bounds around the room and is never still in not particularly desirable either. And beware of "spinners!" These are the dogs or puppies that have become neurotic from being kept in cramped quarters or in crates all the time. When released at last, they run in circles and behave in a most emotionally unstable manner. Puppies with this kind of traumatic background seldom ever regain full composure or adjustment to an "outside" world. The puppy which has had the proper exercise and appropriate, required living quarters will have a normal, spirited, interested outlook on life and will do his utmost to win you over without having to go into a tailspin.

This three-month-old litter was sired by Ch. Bjorneholms Pif out of Ch. Tangra v. Tschomo-Lungma and was bred in West Germany by Mrs. Erika Geusendam. They were whelped in the United States at the home of Rev. and Mrs. D. Allan Easton. The first puppy on the left grew up to become the celebrated winner Ch. Chumulari Ying-Ying.

If the general behavior and appearance of the dog appeals to you, it is time for you to observe him more closely for his physical attributes. First of all, you can't expect to find the long coat that the adult dog eventually acquires—thanks to the many fine modern grooming aids and lots of tender loving care from devoted owners! But needless to say, the healthy puppy's coat should have a nice shine to it, and the thicker the better on the young Shih Tzu.

Look for clear, dark, sparkling eyes, free of discharge. Dark eye rims or lids are indications of good pigmentation and important to your future breeding program—or even general pleasing, good looks. From the time the puppy first opens his eyes until he is about three months old, however, it must be remembered that the eyes have a slight bluish cast to them. The older the puppy, the darker the eye, and always when checking eye color ascertain the age of the dog if you have any doubt in your mind.

When selecting a puppy it is wise to take an experienced breeder with you. If this is not possible, take the Shih Tzu Standard with you and try to interpret it after you have studied one or more puppies in the litter.

With the Shih Tzu the bite is to be especially considered. Check it carefully. Even though the puppy will get another complete set of teeth somewhere between four and seven months of age, there will be some indication of their final position even at this tender age.

The gums should be a good healthy pink in color, and the teeth even now, should be a clear, clean white. Any brown cast to them could mean distemper, either recently or at an earlier age and would count seriously against the puppy in the show ring.

Puppies take anything and almost everything into their mouths to chew on at this age, and a lot of other infectious diseases start, or are introduced through this canal. And the aforementioned distemper

Ch. Mao-Mao of Lhakang nursing her own litter of four gold and whites and a gold "intruder" from her daughter's litter. Although Mao-Mao was a large specimen she was also an excellent producer and in one of her litters she produced no less than four champions.

teeth will stay that way. Also, the puppy's breath should not be sour or unpleasant. This acrid odor can be a result of a poor mixture of food in the diet, or too-low quality of meat, especially if fed raw. Many people have compared the breath of a healthy puppy to that of fresh toast or being vaguely reminiscent of garlic. At any rate, a puppy should never be fed just table scraps, but should have a well-balanced diet containing a good dry dog meal, and a good grade of fresh meat. Poor meat, or too much cereal, or fillers, will only tend to make a dog fat, and while we like our Shih Tzu well-covered and sturdy, we do not want fat dogs!

Needless to say, the puppy should be clean. The breeder or owner who shows you a dirty puppy is one to steer away from at all costs! Look closely at the skin. Make sure it is not covered with insect bites or red, blotchy sores or dry scales. The vent area around the tail should not show evidences of diarrhea or inflammation. By the same

Zizi's Leidza-Tzu, owned by Mrs. Anna-Lisa Vanhanen and bred by Mrs. Ruth Laakso. Sire: Finnish and Norwegian Ch. Marinas Muff-Lung-Feng; dam: Scandinavian Ch. Zizi's Lhamo.

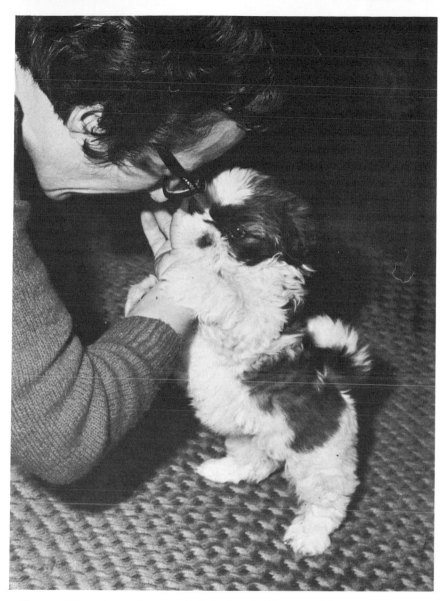

One would have to go a long way to find a breed with as delightful a disposition as that of the Shih Tzu. As puppies they combine the mischievous irresistibility of canine youth with the royal dignity that is their ancient heritage.

token, the puppy's fur should not be matted with dried excrement or smell of urine. True enough, you can wipe dirty eyes, clean dirty ears, and give the puppy a bath when you get it home, but these are all indications of how the puppy has been cared for during the important formative first months of its life, and this can vitally influence its health and future development. There are many reputable breeders raising many healthy puppies that have been brought up under proper conditions in clean establishments, so why take a chance on a series of veterinary bills and an unnecessarily "retarded" puppy?

ANOTHER THOUGHT ABOUT COLOR

The color of your Shih Tzu is a matter of your own personal

These two puppies are just passing out of the "chrysanthemum" stage and are at the age where Shih Tzu puppies bear a marked resemblance to an Australian Koala Bear. The breed does best with individual attention and is not meant for the humdrum of routine kennel life.

Min Yuenne and Yuanne Shih of Elfann, eight-week-old bitch puppies bred by Miss Evans of England. These two were purchased by Mrs. L. G. Widdrington for the purpose of reducing the size of her stock. Min Yuenne reached an adult weight of nine pounds and became a successful competitor in the ring against Shih Tzu of her own size and larger.

preference. As mentioned elsewhere in this book, a white tip on the tail or a blaze on the nose is highly desirable, and the goldens are believed to be the most cherished in the Orient, but blacks and other color mixtures have not discouraged those of us who adore the Shih Tzu for itself alone, without regard to color or markings. We cannot even state at this time that there is a preference in the show ring for certain colors over others. The spirit and personality of this breed is what has endeared it to the dog fancier rather than its color, and this is fortunate.

The choice of sex in your puppy is also something that must be determined before you attempt to select a puppy. Here again, for the pet owner, the sex that would best suit the family life would be the thing to consider. For the breeder or exhibitor this is another

Mr. Per-Axel Lindblom, Swedish-born Shih Tzu fancier, relaxing with two three-month-old puppies. The gown he is wearing comes from Bhutan and the sword is from Tibet. **Mr. Lindblom** took many of the photographs that appear in this book.

"cup of tea." If you are looking for a stud to establish a kennel, it is essential that you select a dog with both testicles evident, even at an early age. Having a veterinarian determine this is wise at this point, before the sale is finalized. One testicle, or a "monorchid" automatically disqualifies your dog from the show ring, and should eliminate him from any breeding program, though monorchids are capable of reproducing. However, it must be cautioned that monorchids frequently sire dogs with the same condition and to knowingly introduce this into a bloodline is an unwritten sin in the dog fancy. Additionally, a monorchid can sire cryptorchids. These have no visible testicles and are completely sterile. Caught being guilty of this has ruined many a kennel, as well as a bloodline.

Never be afraid to ask pertinent questions about the puppy you intend to buy. Feel free to ask the breeder if you might see the dam

Puppies such as these reflect both their fine breeding and the excellent husbandry that has gone into their upbringing. The individual wishing to buy a Shih Tzu of quality should seek out animals similar to these.

(not only to establish her general health, but appearance as a representative of the breed), but ask what the puppy has been fed and should be fed, ask to see the pedigree, inquire if either the litter or the individual puppy has been registered with the American Kennel Club, how many of the temporary and/or permanent inoculations the puppy has had, and will have to have in the future to assure complete immunity, when and if he has been wormed, and if he's had any serious illnesses, diseases or infections. For your own edification, you might also ask if the puppy has been housebroken. It won't mean too much, because he may have learned where "the spot" was where he now lives, but he will still have to learn where "the spot" is in your house! And we cannot expect too much of them at this

Rev. D. Allan Easton with Chumulari Sheng-Li Che posing before a facsimile of a gentleman who might have kept Shih Tzu during the earlier years of the Manchu Dynasty.

age! Many breeders will paper-train their puppies and this will be helpful until housebreaking training can be started.

A reputable breeder will welcome these questions and voluntarily offer this and additional information, if only to "brag" about the tedious care he has given his litter. A reputable breeder will also sell a puppy on twenty-four hour veterinary approval, and also should present you with veterinary certificates with full particulars and information on the dates and kinds of inoculations the puppy has had to date. The veterinarian will also be able to tell you about the general condition of the puppy and advise you on the possible presence of worms.

THE WORRY OF WORMS

Let us give further attention at this point to the unhappy subject of worms in puppies. Generally speaking, all puppies, even puppies reared in clean quarters, come into contact with worms early in life. To say that you must not buy a puppy because it has worms might mean passing up a quality dog unnecessarily. The presence of worms

Chumulari Nieh Tzu, aged ten weeks, owned by Mrs. Helen Stewart.

has become a relatively minor ailment if not neglected and if treated properly. Here again, it is up to a veterinarian to determine how serious the infestation, the amount of dosage and the appropriate medication to alleviate the situation, and whether or not the dog's general health has been affected to the point of damage.

While your veterinarian is going over the puppy you desire to purchase, you might just as well ask him his opinion of it. While not many veterinarians know all the finer points of each pure breed, they have handled enough dogs in their practice to have "a good eye" for a good specimen and can perhaps give you an additional unbiased opinion. He certainly can point out serious structural or organic faults common to all breeds, its general good health, and the finer points of the breed he should be able to count on you to point out to him as a result of your preliminary research and observations on the breed.

The Shih Tzu's friendliness and his natural desire to be with people give him a keen interest in everything that goes on in the home. This group of house dogs are observing young Andrew Easton in a pea-shelling session.

A new puppy requires that the owner be conscious of its important needs. The breeder can envision the perfect mating, and take care to see that the dam is well taken care of and that the puppies have the best possible start in life, but it falls to the new owner to make sure that feeding, training and veterinary attention are not neglected for the life-long well-being of the dog he acquires.

We might mention here that only through the close cooperation of breeder or owner and the veterinarian can we expect to reap the harvest of modern research. Most reputable veterinarians are more than anxious to learn and we in turn must acknowledge and apply what they have proven after much research and practical experience in their field. We can buy or breed the best dog in the world, but when disease strikes we are only as safe as our veterinarian is capable —so let us never hesitate to keep him informed breed by breed— dog by dog. Never underestimate the value of a good veterinarian. They can mean the difference between life and death! And they can certainly point out whether or not a dog is basically cow-hocked, emaciated, under weight, roach-backed, sway-backed or is in general, in good health. His general "over-hauling" and observations, will be

Chumulari Ying Su with her mistress, Miss Gail Marcus. This very attractive pair helped bring the Shih Tzu to a vast national audience when they were selected for special prominence in a feature story on the breed in LIFE magazine's July 11th, 1969 issue.

Too many in-between-meal snacks are not a good idea, but a dog biscuit during the day helps a puppy along to pass the time.

one of the best investments you will ever make in connection with buying a new puppy.

While it is customary for you to pay for the puppy before you take it away with you, if there is any doubt a deposit should suffice. You might post-date a check to cover the twenty-four hour veterinary approval. And if you do decide to keep the puppy the breeder is required to supply you with a pedigree along with the puppy and the ownership papers when the check is cashed. And to supply you with complete information and instruction on how to register your puppy with the American Kennel Club.

Many breeders will offer buyers time payment plans for buying convenience if the purchase price is large if you assure the seller it is a condition of sale. These terms must be worked out individually between buyer and seller—and always in writing to avoid later entanglements and questions. You will find most breeders to be cooperative if they believe you are sincere in your love for the puppy and will give it the proper home and/or exposure in the show ring if it is a worthy specimen of the breed.

CHAPTER VI

GROOMING THE SHIH TZU

All dogs, but especially the long-coated breeds such as the Shih Tzu, require regular, careful grooming. A beautifully-coated dog which wears proudly the thick, luxurious coat you've taken the time and trouble to cultivate is a joy to behold, both in and out of the show ring. Once ruined or let go almost beyond repair, the coat takes endless time and energy to restore to its original natural lustre and length. It is wise to take a little time each day to keep your dog in top condition rather than try to repair the damage that has been done by accumulated neglect. This is especially true if a dog is to be presented in the show ring.

To establish grooming as a common practice in the daily routine, you'll find matters simplified by choosing a particular spot for grooming your dog each time. You'll make it easier for yourself by placing the grooming table where the light is good and where the dog will have the least distractions. If you are grooming for the show ring it will be wise to set aside a time for grooming each and every day to keep the coat in top condition rather than let it go and then try to "catch up" as the show dates roll around. Eliminate temptations by keeping toys, dog biscuits, other dogs or family pets, etc., out of sight. Make the dog know there is work to be done and that you mean to do it. Be firm—but gentle—about it.

How you choose to position your dog for grooming is a matter of choice for your own convenience. Just remember that surface grooming is never enough. You must groom from the skin to the ends of the hair if your efforts are to be effective. Just be sure that while the dog is on a grooming table that it be steady. Dogs are always nervous about their footing and the table should be firmly planted on the floor. A ribbed rubber matting on the grooming table is best for the surface and is still easy to clean.

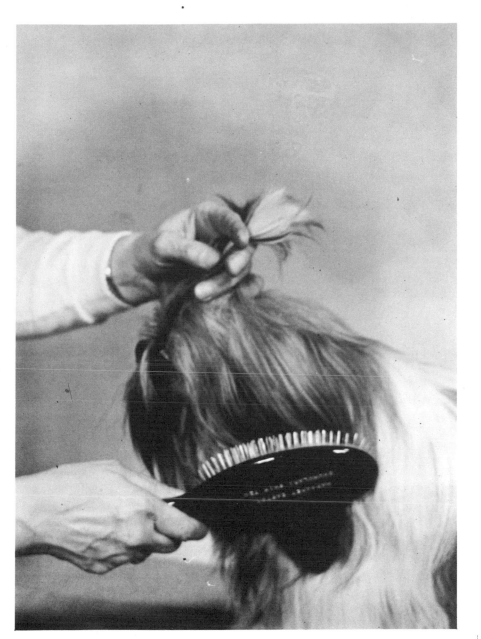

Daily grooming is essential to the well-being of the Shih Tzu. Regardless of whether your dog is a show animal or a housepet, his coat requires regular, careful attention. In this photograph the operator is holding the topknot in place with one hand while brushing down the balance of the face furnishings with the other. A pin brush is considered best for Shih Tzu grooming.

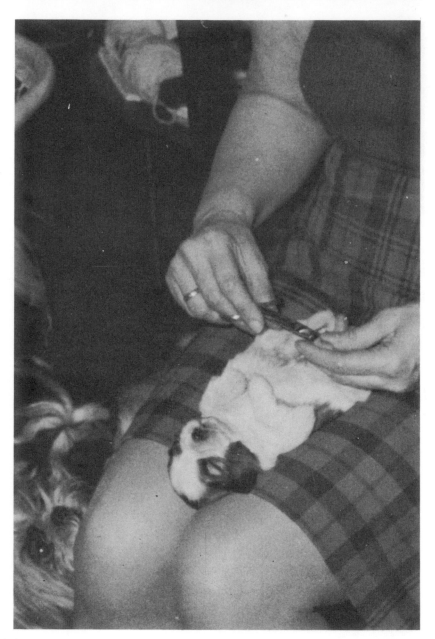

It is important to keep the tiny nails of very young puppies trimmed short. By the age of six weeks a puppy should have had its nails trimmed at least twice. The best way to hold a young puppy when trimming nails is in your lap on its back. Styptic powder or a similar coagulant should always be handy in the event that one nail is cut too short and there is bleeding.

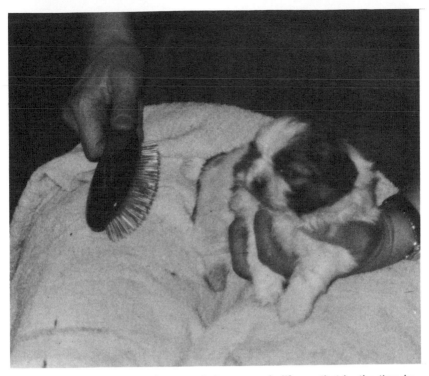

Grooming should be started very early in a puppy's life, so that by the time he is grown he will behave properly during grooming sessions. This five-week-old puppy is being introduced to this important aspect of a Shih Tzu's life by gentle use of the pin brush.

There is no set amount of time recommended for grooming to produce the desired effect. Dogs that are more heavily coated will naturally require more time. But enough time should be allotted for going over the entire dog each time it is put on the grooming table. What you skip over one time would be twice as hard to remedy by the next time, and you always run the risk of pulling out twice as much hair when a certain spot has been allowed to get twice as tangled! These spots that you have missed will show up all too frequently, and this simply will not do for a show dog!

The correct brush for the Shih Tzu should have pin bristles and coat should be brushed in layers from the skin out to the very ends of the hair. If your brush is gathering hair on one side only, you are not holding it properly. The coat should be brushed in the direction

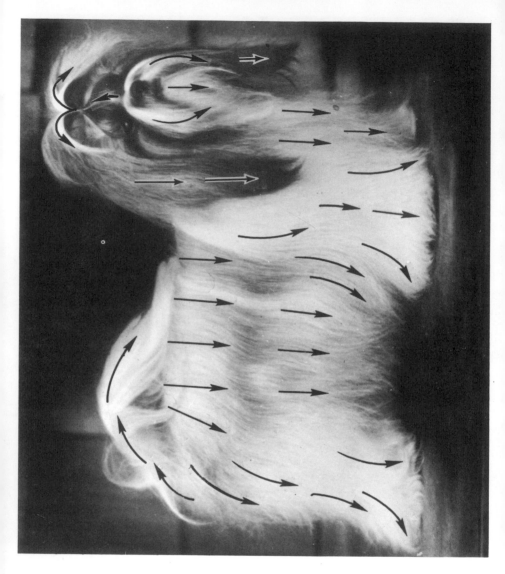

SHIH TZU GROOMING CHART
Arrows indicate the direction in which the coat should be brushed.

in which the coat is to fall. See our visual diagram with arrows indicating the direction in which it should be brushed. The top knot should be brushed up and a rubberband doubled over two fingers with the hair pulled through it, making sure that the hair is not pulled too tightly back over the eyes so as to pull the lids away from the eye sockets or making blinking of the eyes difficult.

The one exception to the grooming of the coat in the direction in which it is to fall is for puppies. Here the method of brushing the coat "every which way" does the hair itself no actual harm and stimulates the skin and hair cells to encourage growth of the permanent coat. Also the legs can be fluffed up before the last minute finishing touches as well.

Special attention should also be given to the feet. The feet are usually the first part of the dog to get dirty. Therefore, they are also

No part of the Shih Tzu coat should be overlooked during a grooming session. Mats and tangles are difficult to overcome once they have been allowed to become established, so the best way of coping with mats is never to let them get started in the coat to begin with.

usually the first spots to get tangled and matted. The hocks and elbows should receive special attention since bones are prominent in these areas and friction and wear can cause holes in the coat.

Should you find a bad tangle or mat, brush away the surrounding hair and take the mat in your hand. Take a little bit of mat at a time and shred it gently with your fingers, working it apart. Then take a comb and carefully and gently work it out from the ends of the hair first until you get up to the skin. Start at the bottom and work up toward the body. When the mat has all been separated, start brushing the broken hairs out gently until all the remaining hairs are free. Then you are ready to brush it back into the rest of the coat.

There are various kinds of grooming aids and coat conditioners that can help you keep your dog well groomed and smelling like a rose. They are on sale at all pet shops and at the concession booths at all dog shows. Consult the breeder of the puppy you buy to learn

The coats of young puppies such as these may be brushed in any direction, and the stimulation to coat and skin from such brushing is beneficial. With the adult coat it is important to brush with the grain only. To do otherwise can result in serious coat damage.

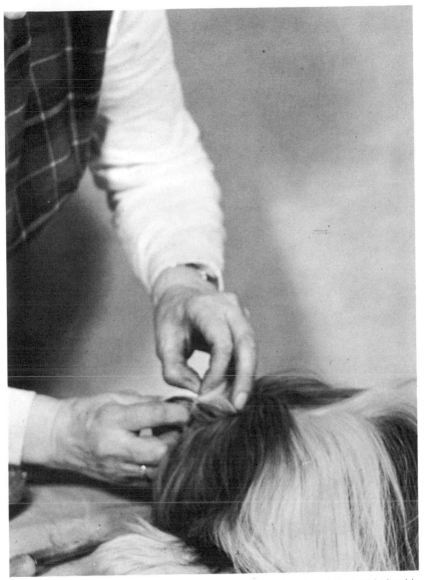

The Shih Tzu's topknot is held in place with a rubber band, and the band should be cut off and replaced with a fresh one daily. Some fanciers use small "pony-tail" barets to keep the topknots up at home and save rubber bands for the show ring. The use of hair ribbons as in some other of the longhaired toy breeds is not advisable because it would tend to detract from the otherwise typically Chinese expression.

A Shih Tzu puppy is usually old enough for a topknot by the time it is about five months old. It is at this same time that the face furnishings begin to develop to give the dog his distinctly oriental expression. For a time during this period a Shih Tzu puppy bears a striking resemblance to an Australian Koala Bear.

which he or she has been most successful with and you will usually find that you have been given good advice. Naturally, if your dog tends toward dry skin you would prefer a dressing with an oil base. These are applied with an atomizer as you groom and are brushed into the coat.

If your Shih Tzu is outdoors a great deal or lives in a city where soot and excessive street dirt plagues him, you will more than likely want to use one of the dry shampoos or lather dry baths between actual tub baths. But do not expect miracles from these man-made preparations. Only *you* with proper grooming and proper feeding will maintain the good health that will normally give your Shih Tzu the lustrous coat it is meant to have.

GROOMING BEHAVIOR

If your Shih Tzu wiggles and squirms and backs off and fights you every bit of the way when grooming time rolls around, chances are you're being a little too rough. True enough, there are dogs that just never do get to like being groomed, and these dogs require extra patience and, quite possibly, extra work, since they will employ every scheme known to canines to put you off and hamper your progress. But more than likely if you meet resistance it's because the dog is genuinely uncomfortable.

The main thing is to be gentle; be even more gentle in the sensitive areas such as the groin, the feet, under the tail, around the eyes, etc. The calmest of dogs will flinch when he sees the bristles of a brush or the shiny teeth of a steel comb flashing overhead. You can be pretty brisk on the body, and chest, but such fervor in the tender regions can resemble the Chinese torture!

Since we are dealing with a long-coated breed it will pay off later on to get him to like being groomed right from the time he is a puppy. So concentrate on doing the right job while you're making sure you're doing a good job of grooming. Grooming will probably never seem easy, but it can be a gratifying experience for both dog and master if approached with common sense and patience. Let your dog see that you take a definite pride in taking care of him. He will appreciate this interest and gentleness and attention, and it will result in a closer communication between you and your dog through this personal relationship. And he'll certainly look more beautiful with the right care!

CHAPTER VII

BATHING YOUR SHIH TZU

There are probably as many theories on how, and how often, to bathe a dog as there are dog owners. There is, however, no set rule or frequency or method, although it is certain that show dogs, or dogs that are outdoors a great deal in all kinds of weather and still spend time indoors with the family, will require a bath on occasion.

Once you've made up your mind that the time for the bath has come, the smartest thing to do is to put a drop or two of mineral oil in your dog's eyes to prevent burning from soap suds that might splash in, and you might also place small wads of cotton in the ears to prevent water from entering them, and to soften the sound of the dryer while he is drying.

With dogs the size of the Shih Tzu you'll find a sink will make bathing easier. The drainage is ideal for the several rinsings that will be necessary, and a hand spray or length of hose can be attached to the faucet where there is adequate water pressure to speed the process.

The successful soaping that will clean your dog thoroughly can best be achieved if your dog is well-drenched with warm water first. Start at the withers with the hose, after letting a little water run in the sink around his feet first, and then work from the withers backwards to the end of the tail. Save the head until very last. You will find the dog stays warmer and is less restless if he gets used to the feel of the water on his body before having the stream of water directed over his eyes.

Once the coat is throughly drenched with water work up a thick lather with one of the richer shampoos. Make sure the soap is lathered in all the way to the skin all over the dog, and be just as sure that after you've lathered him for the second time, that every last bit of shampoo is rinsed out of the coat. Place the stream of water from the hose as close to the skin as possible, separating the

The coat should be thoroughly soaked before and after soaping. A coat that has been made wet will be easier to apply shampoo to and will lather up better. The purpose of a thorough rinsing after the shampoo is to make sure that no soap remains to dull the coat or to produce dandruff or mats.

coat as you move along. Rinsing every last bit of shampoo out of the coat cannot be stressed enough. Any soapy residue that is left behind will make the hair gummy, dull and lifeless, and will dry the skin as well. So it is best to use a wide spray for the rinsing. Start at the head, rinsing down the neck, and over the body. Do not just dump a pail of water over the dog's head. Grasp the muzzle firmly in one hand, tilt the head up and back and let the water run down the head and neck from a point just behind the eyes. The foreface and chin should be done from underneath.

After the head and body are done, the feet and legs should get additional and particular attention, since some of the rinse water remains in the bottom of the tub or doesn't run off quickly enough and will cling to the feet. Rinse them once again until you are convinced the soap has been washed away completely. Then do it once again for good measure!

If you use any kind of conditioner or creme rinse on your dog now is the time to apply it. Then another rinse, and let the dog drip-dry for a minute or two before gathering him up in the towel for an initial drying. Try to avoid using a circular motion with the towel. Long-coated dogs tend to tangle from this and will pose a grooming problem later on. While you are doing this drying with the towel it would be a good idea to start the dryer, not only to get the dog used to the sound of it, but it can be warming up to the desired temperature in the meantime.

When the dryer is ready place the dog on the grooming table and with your brush, start brushing the dog dry, working within the current of warm air. Allow about a foot of space between the dryer and the brush and here again brush in layers in the direction in which the coat is to lie. Try to brush all over the dog so he dries evenly and not just in one spot while the rest is dripping wet. When brushing the feet and legs it is helpful to place the dog's feet at the edge of the table so that you can brush from the skin to the ends of the hair without hitting the table.

Your Shih Tzu should never be allowed to be dry on the outside while remaining wet next to the skin. So don't bathe your dog unless you are fully prepared to finish the job properly once you've started it. Also watch out for drafts or a room that is too cold.

BATHING THE PUPPY

Here again there are two schools of thought on the advisability of

212

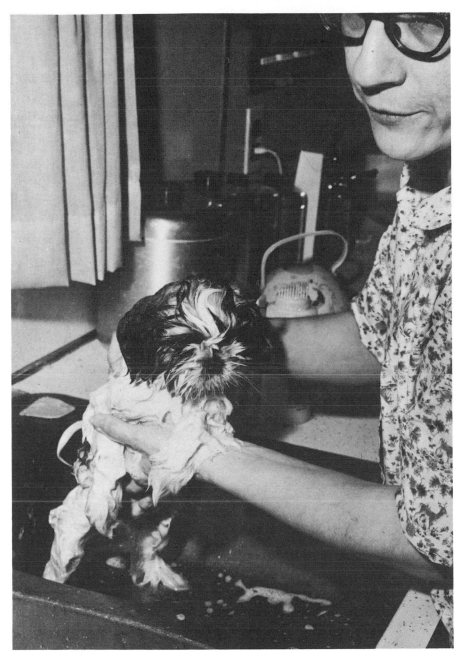

A good-quality, non-matting dog shampoo followed by a cream rinse are necessary elements for the Shih Tzu's bath. Always put a drop of mineral oil in the eyes to protect them and plug the ears with cotton to keep out the water. Care should also be taken so that the dog will not skid in the bath as this can be dangerous to him.

213

bathing the very young puppy. If you are an advocate of the bath, the same technique can be used for the puppy that is advised for the grown dog. Drafts are very dangerous for puppies, and *never* leave a puppy only partially dry.

If you believe a bath exposes and endangers a puppy unnecessarily, it is wise to know about the dry shampoos mentioned earlier when a cleaning job seems advisable. These dry shampoos, plus regular brushings, will keep the puppy reasonably clean as well as stimulate the hair follicles and encourage the natural hair oils for good coat.

Bathing a dog is hard work at best, and if you don't know a few of the tricks of the trade, with a long-haired dog it can be a disaster, with everyone and everything ending up equally wet. We would suggest a rubber apron or an old, lightweight raincoat with the sleeves cut off at the elbows as proper attire because sooner or later your dog is going to shake himself!

CHAPTER VIII

CORRECT CANINE MANAGEMENT

LIVING QUARTERS

In spite of all that is said about the long coat protecting the Shih Tzu from both the sun and the cold, we must caution about the dangers of dampness and violent temperature changes when it comes to the living quarters for your dog. With a heritage of luxurious living in the palaces of the Orient, the domesticated dogs of today for the most part share the lovely homes of their owners in our affluent society but still must be protected against sudden change in

Although the Shih Tzu is classified as a Toy breed he is an energetic companion indoors and out. Here a group of the Chumulari Shih Tzu relax with Mrs. Margaret Easton at the family's Cape Breton, Nova Scotia vacation home.

215

Because of the breed's amiable nature it is possible to keep numbers of dogs together without their quarreling. This group of mixed ages and sexes are perfectly happy to share the same home and the attentions of Andrew and David Easton in play.

temperature or weather conditions. This is particularly true with puppies. While the Shih Tzu is a rugged little dog, it is sheer folly for a dog to sleep indoors by the stove, or beneath a comforter on his master's bed one night, and then be expected to spend the next night outdoors in a dog house or in a drafty garage. Shih Tzu have a way of choosing their own beds, and it will probably be the same as yours!

ENVIRONMENT

Perhaps the most important of all aspects in the care and health of your Shih Tzu is diet! Meat, whether raw or cooked is advisable, and a good meal or kibble, which in itself provides a complete balanced diet, are essential. Fresh water available at all times is also a diet essential. The "extras" you may choose to supplement the diet, or to "treat" your dog, such as egg yolks, wheat germ, calcium supplements, dog biscuits, certain vegetables, tomatoes, and any of the vitamin preparations for dogs, are a matter of choice.

Every breeder will prescribe the diet he or she prefers, and bring you up to date on what the puppy you are buying has been raised on, but if there is any question at all about the diet, your veterinarian is the man to consult. Digestive upsets can retard proper growth in a puppy and be almost as dangerous as its not getting enough food at all.

Since the capacity and size of the individual dog determines the amount of food he should consume each day, we'll not go into quantitative measure in regard to feeding in this book. You can find quite accurate guides according to breed on the labels of most products you buy. In time you will learn your dog's capacity and can feed minimum or maximum measures according to his condition. The common danger for everyone is to overfeed. This can be dangerous, especially in old age. A healthy dog should eat the approximate same amount every day, and will be in good flesh without going to fat. Table scraps of course are out of the question. Dogs need a balanced diet as much as your family does.

As an illustration of the perfectly brought up household, the Chinese tell the story of Ch'en, of the town of Chiang Chou, who not only preserved harmony among the 700 members of his family but also had the family dogs so well trained that, if one was late for dinner, the other 99 waited for him!

No explanation is given how this feat was accomplished, but another Chinese sage, Chang Kung-i of Shantung, has provided us with a clue. Questioned by a T'ang Emperor how he kept nine branches of the family together, Chang gave an answer often quoted in China, by writing one word a hundred times—"jen-mai," meaning "patience" or "forbearance."

The stories are legendary, of course, and there is nothing to suggest that the Ch'en family dogs—if they ever existed—were Shih Tzu Kou. Yet such tales do draw attention to the fact that the Shih Tzu can be trained in obedience since they are highly intelligent, remarkably responsive, and unusually quick to learn.

Their training does call for patience, however, since they have a

Chumulari Woo Muh, C.D., one of the first Shih Tzu to earn a title in all-breed obedience competition. She was trained by Miss Marvel Runkel. The Shih Tzu has proven a very apt pupil in obedience and goes about the exercises with the happy enthusiasm so typical of the breed when he is doing something for and with those he loves.

self-willed streak—a fact to which my attention was drawn by the leading dog trainer in the United States who spoke of the breed with the utmost admiration but emphasized, with a smile, that they could occasionally be very stubborn.

HOUSEBREAKING

House training should begin at a very early age, either on paper or outside, while a small puppy can soon be familiarized with simple commands.

OBEDIENCE TRAINING

It is unwise to take too young a dog to public classes, although these are of great value at a slightly later stage. As puppies vary in their rate of development, every owner must decide for himself when the time for such training has come. Particulars regarding obedience classes, which are becoming increasingly popular, can be obtained from any nearby kennel club or from the local newspapers.

At this writing seven Shih Tzu have attained the coveted degree of "Companion Dog" in the United States. By far the first of these were Si-Kiangs Say-It-Again, trained by Herb Kellogg of Illinois, and Si-Kiangs Puddy Kat, trained by Miss Susan Clinch of Delaware. Both these dogs were bred by the late Mrs. Ingrid Colwell who did so much to introduce into North America top quality Shih Tzu from her native Sweden.

A more recent C.D. is Chumulari Woo Muh whose trainer, Miss Marvel Runkel of Spokane, Washington, has written—"She is so smart and loved her obedience training. The other day I was training my Pekingese and Woo Muh continued to cry until I let her go through all the exercises right along with my Peke."

Exceptionally courageous for their size and doggedly tenacious on occasion, Shih Tzu can make good watch dogs. During the Cyprus troubles of the 1950s, "a nice little Shih Tzu called Tensing," belonging to a British couple, Mr. and Mrs. Roland Morris, was credited with giving the alarm and being "responsible for the cornering and capture of an armed deserter lurking in the grounds which was a great feather in his cap and became an epic."

In view of their exceptionally out-going and friendly nature, however, under normal circumstances Shih Tzu are best regarded as first and foremost dearly loved household pets.

Shih Tzu are extremely photogenic, a fact which is rapidly becoming known to advertising agencies. Some of our Chumulari dogs have appeared more than once on T.V., while others have been featured in the pages of the national press in one capacity or another. As photographers are well aware, a compact Shih Tzu and a pretty girl can make a formidable combination!

On such occasions it is essential that the dog be in good coat and that it be well groomed. Shih Tzu in poor condition, or ill-kept, reflect credit on neither owner nor breed.

Intelligent though Shih Tzu are, it must be acknowledged that there is a limit to their capabilities. Mrs. Widdrington recounts how an exhibitor was once asked at a show: "Are these the Chinese dogs that comb their own hair with their hind claws?" To this the reply must be a regretful negative, although every fancier must sometimes wish that it were true!

Short of such a feat, however, the proud Shih Tzu owner will find his pet astonishingly apt to learn. All that is required is patience, and a genuine bond of affection and understanding between master (or mistress) and dog.

VETERINARY VISITS

Like your dentist, your veterinarian advises that your dog pay him a visit twice a year. Preventative measures can save money by preventing disease from hitting hard with these semi-annual check-ups and booster shots. Especially if you are raising or breeding show dogs, where they will be exposed to so many other strange dogs.

LICENSING

Most towns require a dog license after six months of age. Call your town dog warden to check on requirements for this.

SUBJECT INDEX